FOOD LOVERS'
GUIDE TO THE
TWIN CITIES

Help Us Keep This Guide Up to Date

We would love to hear from you concerning your experiences with this guide and how you feel it could be improved and kept up to date. Please send your comments and suggestions to:

editorial@GlobePequot.com

Thanks for your input, and happy travels!

FOOD LOVERS'
GUIDE TO THE
TWIN CITIES

The Best Restaurants, Markets & Local Culinary Offerings

1st Edition

James Norton

Guilford, Connecticut

Editor: Amy Lyons
Project Editor: Lynn Zelem
Layout Artist: Mary Ballachino
Text Design: Sheryl Kober
Illustrations by Jill Butler with additional art by Carleen Moira Powell and MaryAnn Dubé
Base maps provided by Compass Maps Ltd.
Maps © Morris Book Publishing, LLC

ISBN 978-0-7627-7948-2

Printed in the United States of America
10 9 8 7 6 5 4 3 2 1

All the information in this guidebook is subject to change. We recommend that you call ahead
to obtain current information before traveling.

I dedicate this book to my favorite dining companion: my wife, Becca. I literally couldn't do this without you—it's your terrific palate that tells me when I'm on the right track, and your sense of humor that keeps me relatively sane. Here's to another 60 to 70 years of dining together.

Contents

Regional Gastronomic Info, 177

Food Fests & Events, 225

Three Upper Midwestern Foodie Road Trips, 231

Recipes, 239

Appendices, 261

Index, 278

About the Author

After a career of editing Middle East news at the *Christian Science Monitor* and researching domestic political stories for (now Senator) Al Franken's radio show, Madison, Wisconsin native James Norton shifted gears and began writing food stories after moving from the East Coast to Minneapolis.

He contributed restaurant reviews to *Minnesota Monthly* before picking up a yearlong gig as a reviewer for *City Pages,* the leading alt weekly of the Twin Cities. He is now a contributing columnist to CHOW.com, and the editor of the *Heavy Table*, a daily online magazine dedicated to reporting on the food and drink of the Upper Midwest. Over the past five years, between his various food writing jobs in the Cities, he has eaten at several hundred different restaurants and profiled dozens of chefs, food cart vendors, farmers, cheesemakers, brewers, and other food professionals.

Along with his wife (photographer Becca Dilley) he's the author of *The Master Cheesemakers of Wisconsin,* a book on Minnesota folk food called *Minnesota Lunch: From Pasties to Banh Mi,* and an upcoming book about the food of the Lake Superior region to be published by the University of Minnesota Press. He and Becca live in Minneapolis.

Acknowledgments

I am greatly in debt to my friend Rachel Hutton, who was my editor at *Minnesota Monthly* and my former colleague at *City Pages*; without her help, the doors to the world of food and drink writing in the Twin Cities would have been closed.

I also owe thanks to my colleagues at the *Heavy Table*, whose tireless reviewing, researching, and reporting have greatly enhanced my own understanding of the growing gastronomic scene in the Upper Midwest. The adventure of exploring local food has been far richer for your companionship and insights.

Amy Lyons, my editor at Globe Pequot, has been a delight to work with, and her support and clear guidance have been instrumental in bringing this book to fruition.

And most of all, I owe thanks to my wife, Becca. Her patience, support, and input are, in a word, awesome.

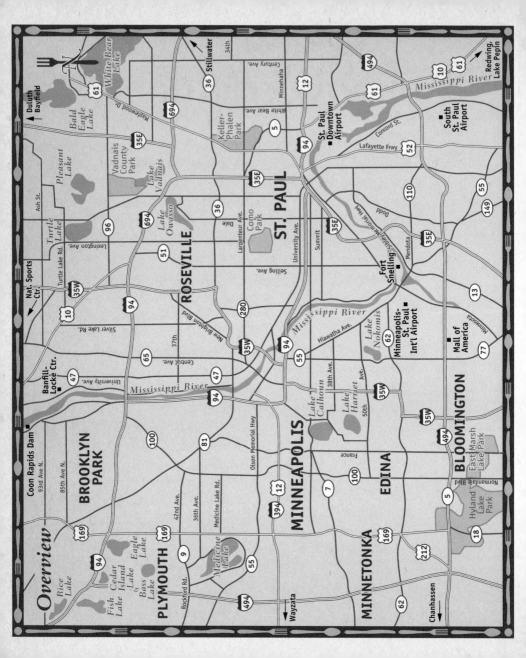

Introduction

In recent years, the twin cities of Minneapolis and St. Paul have been showered with titles dished out by national publications: most literate, most civically engaged, gayest, hippest, and so forth. This fact isn't trotted out to put too much stock in lists designed to pique readers (and irritate New Yorkers), but rather to point out that despite being located near the frozen heart of the Upper Midwest, the Twin Cities have some stuff going on.

Quite a lot of stuff going on, to be precise—the Cities have a thriving art and music scene, access to vast tracts of gorgeous wilderness and quite a few of the state's famous 10,000 lakes, and one of the most exciting food scenes in the country, bar none.

Incredulous? That's fair. But here's the short version of the story (the long version unspools over the course of the rest of this book).

Minneapolis-St. Paul is, like many a fortunately situated French or Italian province, swimming in agriculture. From pork to poultry to Lake Superior fish to cheese to apples to vegetables, the farmers and ranchers of Minnesota, Wisconsin, Iowa, and the Dakotas provide. Granted that much of that agriculture is of the factory farm variety, but two important things are happening:

The first is that Minnesotans are learning how to recognize the best and rarest of what's produced right next door, and the second is that Midwestern farmers, ranchers, and dairymen are learning how to cultivate the heirloom, the flavorful, the premium, and the exotic. The result is an explosion of creativity in a part of the country once best known for flavorless plates of all-white Scandinavian food and stick-to-the-ribs (but not the taste buds) hotdish.

And so, inspired by the Californian eateries that have done so much with the treasures of local agriculture, farm-to-fork restaurants have taken off. There has been a surge in the number of creative gourmet food trucks. Ethnic food (including a good deal of Hmong and Vietnamese offerings, plus some terrifically authentic Mexican and Somali offerings) is learning how to adapt to the local palate without selling out its roots, and the local palate is learning how to eat ethnic food. Tolerance for spicy food has doubled or tripled in the last decade, and while it's still far from robust, it's getting there.

Meanwhile, the old advantages of geography persist. Wild game is commonly available, and more adventurous restaurants take advantage of its exotic flavor, serving up venison, elk, and rabbit. All those lakes and all of the Upper Midwest's clean, clear fresh water means there are plenty of fish to choose from, including some excellent spring-fed farmed trout and fish from Lake Superior. And the land yields other bounty as well: berries, herbs, mushrooms, ramps, and more.

If you explore the Twin Cities restaurant scene with an open mind, you'll discover that it's a clearinghouse for the region as a whole. And that means great craft beer from nearby counties and states, Wisconsin cheese (best in the world according to international medal counts and overwhelming in its variety), and the delights of the North and South shores of Superior: world-class smoked fish and some of the best berry and apple pie in the country.

The key thing is to come in with an open mind and give the chefs and purveyors of the region a chance. The Upper Midwestern food revolution is in full swing, and by visiting now and holding this book in your hands, you're lucky enough to be a part of it.

How to Use This Book

The several hundred restaurants in this book are only a sliver of the several thousand restaurants in the Twin Cities metro area, but they represent much of what is exciting about the food scene here. They are selected for quality, longevity, and/or notoriety, with an emphasis on places that are independently and/or locally owned and, when possible, representative of local traditions, cultures, and ethnic groups.

In the pages that follow, you'll find entries organized for easy navigation. The front half of the book is dedicated to restaurants and divided into two parts: Minneapolis and St. Paul. The back highlights everything from gourmet shops and ethnic grocers to farms worth visiting to recipes.

Throughout the book, you'll find sidebars talking about different aspects of Twin Cities food culture, including food traditions, new ethnic influences, unusual local ingredients, and so forth.

Each listing shows the name of the establishment, address, phone number, website (when available), cuisine type, and price code.

Landmark Eateries

Restaurants that have gained some fame—locally or globally—for their longevity or great food and service are profiled. These are the tried-and-true favorites, iconic restaurants that have made it through tough economic times and withstood the biggest test in the restaurant business—the test of time.

Foodie Faves

From simple taquerias to white-tablecloth bistros to seafood shacks, these eateries are popular with locals and visitors, too. This is a comprehensive restaurant guide that spotlights a wide range of restaurants, from cutting-edge eateries to sophisticated dining rooms and family-owned ethnic spots. Here you will also find the newer, trendier eateries.

Restaurant Price Key

The number of dollar signs indicates what you may expect to pay for an entree and a drink. Due to the large number of restaurants offering small-plate-style dining, this guide is a rough approximation. Whenever possible, we'll indicate when a restaurant allows for flexible dining that means diners can skate out the door with a light check or indulge, full-on, for a sumptuous (and pricey) meal.

$	less than $10
$$	$10 to $20
$$$	$20 to $40
$$$$	$40 or more a plate

Regional Gastronomic Info

In this part you'll find information on everything from specialty stores, locally made regional specialties, food trucks, farms and orchards, local food (& beer) groups, and popular festivals and events.

Recipes

Here you'll find some wonderful recipes from some of the Cities' top chefs.

Three Upper Midwestern Foodie Road Trips

Explore these charming road trips convenient from the Twin Cities that combine good food and natural beauty.

Keeping Up with Food News

The *Star Tribune*'s Rick Nelson is an anchor of the local food writing community—his influence as a restaurant critic is felt statewide, and his style of journalism is clearheaded, thoughtful, down-to-earth, loaded with verified facts, and up-to-date. You can find his work in print, at his paper's online **Taste Section** (startribune.com/lifestyle/taste), and all over the *Star Tribune* website.

Local beer lovers are lucky enough to have a dedicated online resource that is focused on all brew, all the time: **MNBeer** (mnbeer.com) is a rapidly updated and competently written compendium of local beer events, new beer releases, and miscellaneous beer news. The **Captain's Chair** beer blog (captainsbeerblog.com) brings a passionate homebrewer's perspective to the scene, and **A Perfect Pint** (aperfectpint.net/blog.php) is written by Michael Agnew, the state's first certified **Cicerone** (think sommelier, but for beer).

Trout Caviar (troutcaviar.blogspot.com) is the foremost voice of the Upper Midwestern foraging movement, bringing a haute cuisine mentality to a wilderness guide's garden and pantry. It's a collection of essays, opinions, and recipes including everything from a smoked duck salad with local berries to caponata with milkweed relish. The blog's author, Brett Laidlaw, recently published a book called *Trout Caviar: Recipes from a Northern Forager,* and it includes the likes of a Ramps and Fiddlehead Fern Tart and Herring Crudo with Cider Mustard Cream.

The **Heavy Table** (heavytable.com), which I edit, is a daily online journal of Upper Midwestern food that is dedicated to putting shoe-leather reporting back into Web journalism—the site is driven by in-person interviews, restaurant visits, road trips, professional photography, and old-fashioned research. With new stories daily and a running aggregation of stories published in other outlets, it's a good first stop for the curious Upper Midwestern omnivore.

There's an active food blogging scene in the Twin Cities as well. Some of the best include **Eating for England** (eating-for-england .com/), which offers a relatively recent immigrant's perspective on Midwestern eats; the exploits of married gastronomers and gardeners **Martha and Tom** (marthaandtom.com), and the **Well Fed Guide to Life** (fancypantsgangsters.com/shows/wellfed), a podcast taped at a different local restaurant every week. **Stephanie A. Meyer** (who writes at freshtart.net) maintains her own lavishly photographed online presence and also organizes the **Minnesota Food Bloggers,** an umbrella group of local online food writers.

Andrew Zimmern may be a nationally known food television superstar, but he's also a local—his musing on food (both local and global) can be found in the pages (online and actual) of *Mpls.St. Paul Magazine*.

Multiple James Beard Award–winning journalist **Dara Moskowitz Grumdahl** is one of the area's veteran food and drink voices, heading up criticism at *Mpls.St. Paul Magazine* after years of influential opinion brokering at *City Pages* and then *Minnesota Monthly*.

Cooking Classes & Continuing Gastronomic Education

In Minneapolis, one of the best-known temples to all things gastronomic is **Kitchen Window** (3001 Hennepin Ave., Minneapolis MN 55408; 612-824-4417; kitchenwindow.com), located in the trendy-and-getting-spendier Uptown neighborhood. Kitchen Window boasts of having more individual items in stock than any other kitchen store in the country, and you'll soon believe it after wandering its roomy and well-organized aisles. Staff are well-trained and helpful, and the store boasts well-stocked sections dedicated to knives, cookbooks, coffee and tea, and what is likely the best selection of backyard grills and smokers in the Upper Midwest. As an added bonus, Kitchen Window puts racks of discounted kitchen wares outside of its doors in Calhoun Mall. Beyond gadgets and cookware, Kitchen Window offers one of the most ambitious slates of classes in the Twin Cities area, with everything from Cooking Fundamentals and Knife Skills to Fundamentals of Modern Sauces and Grillmasters: Green Egg Cooking, taught on the notoriously expensive and much-beloved Green Egg gourmet grill. Class fees tend to be high (anywhere from $65 and upward is typical), but quality is also high and classes often include food and/or cookware with the cost of tuition.

Cooks of Crocus Hill (77 Grand Ave., St. Paul, MN 55105; 651-228-1333, and 3925 W. 50th St., Edina, MN 55424; 952-285-1903; cooksofcrocushill.com) may be the closest thing to a rival Kitchen Window has, and while neither of its two locations equals Kitchen Window in terms of sheer size, they command enviable locations (in swanky Edina and St. Paul's cosmopolitan Grand Avenue) and stock an enchanting range of upscale food, cooking utensils, cookware, and all things gastronomic, including seasonal local food crop shares that offer some of the best (and priciest) local food money can buy in the

Upper Midwest. *Minnesota Monthly* called Cooks "the Cadillac of cooking schools," and prices and options reflect that. Priced competitively with Kitchen Window ($65 and up is typical), topics range from Chinese Supper Club to Pub Food and Pints to Wine Pairing with Chef Tyge Nelson to the World Tour of Pork with renowned local charcuterie artist Mike Phillips.

The **Mississippi Market Natural Foods Co-ops** (622 Selby Ave., St. Paul, MN 55104; 651-310-9499, and 1500 W. 7th St., St. Paul, MN 55102; 651-690-0507; msmarket.coop) are a bird of a different feather; while Kitchen Window and Cooks court the Martha Stewart demographic, the Market is a bit more granola. Like a number of their co-op peers in the Cities (the Seward and Linden Hills co-ops come immediately to mind), Mississippi Market is a break from the grungy, sometimes insufferably preachy co-op of the past—it's clean, wide-aisled, and welcoming, and its classes are pitched toward the earnest community member who is as interested in eating healthily and sustainably as eating well. From Homebrewed Root Beer to Cooking with Miso Soup to Vegetarian & Vegan Holiday Dishes, classes appeal to canners, gardeners, and natural food enthusiasts, and tend to range in price from $20 to 30. Members receive a discount on that price, and if you're going to be in the Twin Cities for more than a year, membership in a co-op is an investment that will easily pay for itself.

The expansive and elegant **Chef's Galley of Stillwater** (324 S. Main St., Stillwater, MN 55082; 651-351-1144; thechefsgallery.com) offers classes that are only a bit less expensive ($50 to $60 is typical) than its peers in the Twin Cities and trend a bit more toward homey comfort food (think pies, holiday cookies, cake decorating, homemade candies). If you're touring the Stillwater/Hudson area, it's well worth a visit.

Minnesota Monthly runs the **TC Taste** group food blog (minnesota monthly.com/media/Blogs/Twin-Cities-Taste). It's populated by a number of influential locals, including WCCO reporter and anchor **Jason DeRusha,** who has become a gastronomic force to be reckoned with in his own right. The wry, observant, often deadpan DeRusha blogs, does video, and writes but may be easiest to track and follow via his Twitter account, @DeRushaEats.

Writing from Bemidji, Minnesota, for *The Pioneer,* writer **Sue Doeden** (sdoeden.areavoices.com) captures the taste of outstate Minnesota better than anyone else currently at work in the field. Her homespun recipes always tell a story, and they feature mouth-watering photography as well.

And if you know local food in the Twin Cities, you probably know **The Two Stephanies**—Stephanie March writes about food for *Mpls.St. Paul Magazine* (her Friday Foodie File roundups are a staple found at blogs.mspmag.com/foodiefile), and Stephanie Hansen works with March to create a food-focused show called **Weekly Dish for 107.1** (mytalk1071.com/shows/weeklydish).

Minneapolis

Always seen as the livelier of the two Twin Cities, Minneapolis is the arts and commerce powerhouse, happy to cede government to its neighbor to the east. The city is geographically spread out, and before you decide what you want to eat, it's often helpful to decide where you want to eat. Uptown is packed with trendy nightspots and sushi joints, visually splashy and pulsing with youth and life. Downtown has some of the best high-end luxury and business spots, and its Nicollet Mall is chock-a-block with street food vendors when the weather is accommodating. Many of the city's food-forward gastronomic gems are in the ritzy south-west (particularly the Kingfield neighborhood), where the quiet of this relatively residential area meets the moneyed class of the southwest suburbs. And the Warehouse District (near downtown) is home to some of the most exciting food-forward places to eat, restaurants good enough to prosper proximate to the heart of the city, but not so aggressively priced or otherwise profitable to demand prime downtown real estate.

Minneapolis Landmarks

Al's Breakfast, 413 14th Ave. Southeast, Minneapolis, MN 55414; (612) 331-9991; Breakfast; $$. Take a tight-squeeze alley in U of M's Dinkytown neighborhood, throw a tin-shed-style hut into it and put in a long flattop griddle, and you've got the institution known as Al's Breakfast. Al's serves up gorgeously chewy and perfectly cooked pancakes and comforting bacon-and-eggs-driven breakfast entrees, many of which were likely enjoyed the day the restaurant opened in 1950. There are only 14 stools in the place, but that adds to the considerable charm—by the time you finally grace one of them, you've queued up in a line along the back of the tiny restaurant, looking enviously over the shoulders of those who have come before you as they happily wolf down their chow. Two key things to know before you go: It's a cash-only joint, and there's often a line out the door. The line moves quickly (this is not a place to sit

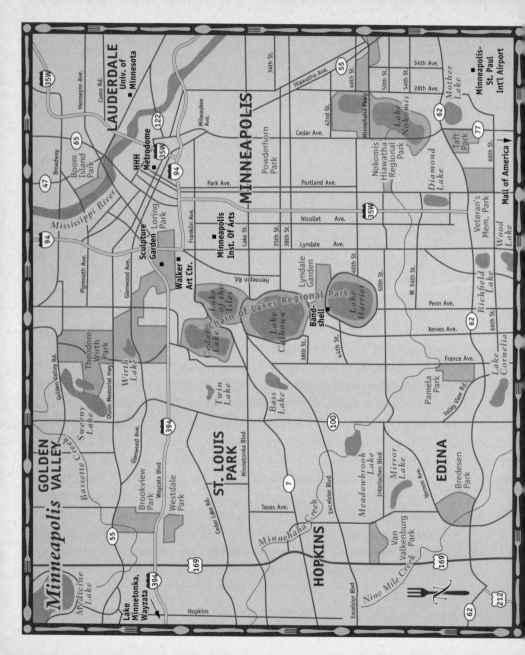

and linger over your coffee), but once you're seated be prepared to move around to a different barstool to accommodate incoming groups. Speaking of which: Al's is best for a group of one, or two. Three is literally a crowd, and if you come with four people, prepare for your group to be broken in half. That's the game you have to play if you want to taste what are likely the best pancakes in the Upper Midwest.

Andrea Pizza, 11 LaSalle Ave., Highland Court Building, Minneapolis, MN 55402; (612) 630-2882; andreampls.com; Pizza; $. OK, so it's not New York—not quite. But even a New Yorker would forgive you for being fooled about the origin of the floppy, foldable, satisfying, hand-tossed pizza pie served up by Andrea Pizza; while not pretending to take on the mantle of the City's truly great pizzerias, the lunch-only shops do a bang-up job of evoking the "slice" that is the mainstay of NYC's lunch on the go. Part of it is the gritty but cheerful atmosphere, and part of it is the longevity of the franchise—the three-restaurant chain dates back to a store called Figaro's that opened in 1972. Andrea Pizza is a unique part of the often unfortunate Minneapolis Skyway ecosystem—a Skyway-based restaurant that offers cheap, authentic food that evokes something other than corporate food service. **Additional locations:** 330 S. 2nd Ave., Towle Building, Minneapolis, MN 55401; (612) 332-6457; 380 Jackson St., Galtier Plaza, St. Paul, MN 55101; (651) 228-1626.

Annie's Parlour, 313 14th Ave. Southeast, Minneapolis, MN 55414; (612) 379-0744; Diner; $$. Malts and burgers are the workhorses at this campus soda parlor–style restaurant located in a spacious room on the second floor of a busy stretch of 14th Avenue in Dinkytown. One of those horses (the burgers) is mostly dead due to regular over-cooking and unremarkable meat, but the thick, flavorful malts are worth enjoying, and even come half in a glass, and half in the frosted metal mixing cup, as is well and proper. It's best used as a dessert option on campus, and it serves that function well, with plenty of space for visitors to relax over a malt and/or coffee and catch up.

Band Box Diner, 729 S. 10th St., Minneapolis, MN 55404; (612) 332-0850; Diner; $. Hearty breakfasts with large, cake-y pancakes (if you happen to like that sort of thing) and classic American diner hamburgers make the vintage Band Box a throwback to a simpler era of dining. A house special known as the Sloppy Bro merits explo-ration by burger nuts in search of a new twist—this less-sloppy sloppy joe features a chopped-up burger patty and green pepper, onions, and sauce, plus cheese. The Band Box is incongruously located not far from the Metrodome in downtown Minneapolis, and its tiny dining room is as long on retro charm as its food is full of feel-good attitude. Or perhaps that's grease. No matter. As downtown breakfast options go, it's one of the more soulful options avail-able, and the food's cheap—particularly compared to the downtown average.

Birchwood Cafe, 3311 E. 25th St., Minneapolis, MN 55406; (612) 722-4474; birchwoodcafe.com; New American; $$. One of the best examples of a neighborhood restaurant that transcends its neighborhood, the Birchwood Cafe has picked up a regional reputation for its use of in-season, local ingredients and its sensitivity to vegetarian, vegan, and gluten-free diners. Its slogan is "good real food," and its menu backs that up, with its emphasis on produce, local when possible, and simple dishes such as sandwiches, pizzas (available gluten-free), and lasagnas. The restaurant also does a series of events including local cookbook authors, special dinners, opportunities to order local meat and produce, and "meet the artist" receptions. The atmosphere is bright and homey, neighborhood-y in the best possible sense of the word—a perfect place for a laid-back evening out or a quick lunch. The restaurant is also known for its tricked-out waffles, which change on a regular basis—a recent version included sweet potatoes, chevre, parmesan, and bacon with a quince chutney and ginger honey butter.

Brit's Pub & Eating Establishment, 1110 Nicollet Mall, Minneapolis, MN 55403; (612) 332-3908; britspub.com; British; $$. From Scotch eggs to fish and chips to battered sausage rolls, the full majestic weight of the British empire's pub food is brought to bear on visitors to Brit's Pub. This sprawling complex of drinkery and games faithfully imports the conviviality of the UK to the milk-fed confines of the Upper Midwest. English ales and locally made Crispin cider define the drink list at Brit's, which is locally known for its high teas and its rooftop entertainments, which include a Garden Park bar and a 10,000-square-foot lawn bowling green. Inconsistent service can be a problem, but generally after two or three Harps or Basses, the worries float away.

The Black Forest Inn, 1 E. 26th St., Minneapolis, MN 55404; (612) 872-0812; blackforestinnmpls.com; German; $$. While Minnesota is known nationally as a Scandinavian hotbed (thanks, *Golden Girls*), it's home to many descendants of German settlers as well. German food traditions are manifested in the state's robust craft brewing culture and also in its old-school traditional German restaurants—**Gasthof Zur Gemutlichkeit** (p. 27) in Northeast Minneapolis, the **Glockenspiel** (p. 146) in St. Paul, and the Black Forest Inn on Eat Street (Nicollet Avenue). Opened by a German immigrant in 1965, the Black Forest is particularly adept at combining the old (bratwurst and kraut, spaetzel and sauerbraten gravy, the ever-popular wiener schnitzel) with the new—the restaurant's Oktoberfest often features specials such as a feast derived from exotic offal meats, or raffles where the prize is membership in a local farm CSA. Ask about the bullet-ridden Richard Avedon photograph hanging near the bar (blackforestinnmpls.com/pgs/art .php)—it's a conversation piece that no other area restaurant can match.

Broders' Cucina Italiana, 2308 W. 50th St., Minneapolis, MN 55410; (612) 925-3113; broders.com/cucina-italiana; Italian; $$. As the deli side of the Broders' Italian mini-empire, Broders' Cucina Italiana offers diners the opportunity to dine in a workaday miniature dining room or take out their orders of big, meaty sandwiches or a variety of Italian side dishes and salads. Italian butter cookies imported from a New Jersey deli are a nice touch, both visually and flavorwise, and the shop also sells a small but well-curated selection of olive oils, balsamic vinegars, cheeses, desserts, and kitchenwares. Pasta sauces and fresh pastas are also available for those who want to swoop in and purchase the fixings for a comforting Italian meal at home.

Broders' Pasta Bar, 5000 Penn Ave. South, Minneapolis, MN 55419; (612) 925-9202; broders.com; Italian; $$. If you're going to eat at just one Italian restaurant in the Twin Cities during your visit, this may be the one—while profoundly non-pretentious and very reasonably priced, Broders' Pasta Bar dishes up some of the tastiest, heartiest, most satisfying and most rave-able Italian food in the area. The house-made fresh-cooked egg noodles that form the base of many of the restaurants' best pastas are toothsome and a delightful canvas upon which ingredients such as prosciutto di Parma, truffle pesto, balsamic vinegar, mascarpone, wild boar, and more can be shown off to their true potential. There are no reservations here (for good and ill), so show up early if you can—the combination of good food and low prices means that the Pasta Bar tends to fill up early and stay busy for the duration.

Bryant Lake Bowl, 810 W. Lake St., Minneapolis, MN 55408; (612) 825-3737; bryantlakebowl.com; Hipster Bistro and Bowling Alley; $$. Bryant Lake Bowl represents a stone-cold brilliant reinvention of a neighborhood bowling alley by Twin Cities restaurant maven Kim Bartmann. Without sacrificing the charming old lanes (you can still bowl at the Bowl), she's introduced locally sourced, sustainable food, a rotating series of events at the attached theater space, and an Uptown hipster vibe that keeps the restaurant packed and popular even amid stiff competition from would-be usurpers. Its breakfast is among the best in town: primally satisfying dishes such as house-made biscuits and mushroom gravy, granola pancakes, custom scrambles, and a classic eggs Benedict make this an ideal place to fuel up after a night of hard partying, and the four available varieties of Bloody Marys make it an ideal place to continue that hard partying into the morning hours. The wake-up beer (Guinness plus a shot of espresso) is recommended only for the bold.

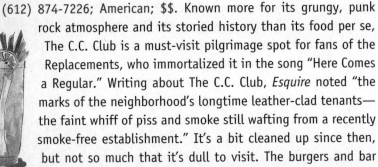

The C.C. Club, 2600 Lyndale Ave. South, Minneapolis, MN 55408; (612) 874-7226; American; $$. Known more for its grungy, punk rock atmosphere and its storied history than its food per se, The C.C. Club is a must-visit pilgrimage spot for fans of the Replacements, who immortalized it in the song "Here Comes a Regular." Writing about The C.C. Club, *Esquire* noted "the marks of the neighborhood's longtime leather-clad tenants— the faint whiff of piss and smoke still wafting from a recently smoke-free establishment." It's a bit cleaned up since then, but not so much that it's dull to visit. The burgers and bar food are passable, but it has in recent years picked up a reputation as a hangover-busting breakfast option with a Bloody Mary hair-of-the-dog option for those who want to keep the party rolling.

Crescent Moon Bakery, 2339 Central Ave. Northeast, Minneapolis, MN 55418; (612) 782-0169; crescentmoonfoods.net; Bakery/Pizza Shop/Afghan; $$. An underground favorite, Crescent Moon Bakery is known to locals by a quick two-word shorthand: "Football pizza." Served on naan-like Afghan flatbread shaped, yes, vaguely like a football, the football pizza is cheap (and/or huge, however you choose to view it), often topped with a hearty halal ground beef, and accompanied by a kicky herbal green chutney that changes the traditional tomato/cheese/meat balance of a pizza to something distinctly more Afghan. Atmosphere at either shop is nothing to write home about, but it's clean and simple, and a fine place to grab a casual but memorable meal with a friend. And if football pizza isn't your thing, Crescent Moon is also well-regarded for its gyros, and baklava makes a nice post-meal kicker. **Additional location:** 1517 Como Ave. SE, Minneapolis, MN; (612) 767-3313.

Dave's Popcorn, 1848 E. 38th St., Minneapolis, MN 55407; (612) 743-6316; davespopcorn.com; Popcorn; $. A trip to the seasonally open Dave's Popcorn (which vends its product from May through October) is one of the classic summer delights of the Powderhorn neighborhood in South Minneapolis. Ice cream, shaved ice, and hot dogs are all on offer, but the big draw is the popcorn—everything from plain to chocolate to herb to house favorite Triple Mix, which combines cheese popcorn with caramel corn and white corn. Seating is outdoors, prices are very low, and it's hard to get more local in spirit and flavor.

Dusty's Bar, 1319 Marshall St. Northeast, Minneapolis, MN 55413; (612) 378-2118; dustysbaranddagos.com Pub; $$. If you're not a regular at Dusty's Bar, you'll know it—everyone in this care-worn, working-class tavern will take a moment to stop and stare at you on your way in, and you'll wonder if you're in the right place. After that, everyone moves on with their lives, and you get to figure out what to drink (Grainbelt Premium is a recommended choice for those who seek to blend in) and eat (probably a hot dago sandwich, just known as a "dago" around here). In St. Paul, hot dagos range from somewhat sloppy to almost lasagna like, big pieces of bread holding a sausage patty slathered in red sauce and cheese—here in Northeast Minneapolis, at Dusty's, the dago is more like a burger with a sausage patty subbed in for the hamburger itself. It's utterly civilized, and can be eaten with one hand and no napkins. And if you really want to take a bite of Northeast, it's this or **Mayslack's** (p. 34).

Fat Lorenzo's, 5600 Cedar Ave. South, Minneapolis, MN 55417; (612) 822-2040; fatlorenzos.com; Italian; $$. The owners of Fat Lorenzo's don't advertise, preferring to trade on a combination of word of mouth, the sponsorship of church suppers, and $10 gift certificates circulated to friends of friends and neighbors. The strategy works: This neighborhood pizzeria bedecked with whimsically Michelangelo-inspired murals is rarely less than packed with folks who clamor for the restaurant's soulful, saucy Midwestern pizza, big beautifully hearty grinders, and house-made gelato. Those who skip the pizza are advised to consider the garlic chicken hoagie, a balanced and profoundly meaty sub that can feed two standard-size adults, and a failure to try the gelato is an unpardonable oversight. **Additional location:** Everett McClay VFW Post 1296, 311 W. 84th St., Bloomington, MN 55420; (952) 854-1296.

5-8 Club Tavern & Grill, 5800 Cedar Ave. South, Minneapolis, MN 55417; (612) 823-5858; 5-8club.com; Burgers; $$. Along with its rival **Matt's Bar** (p. 34), the 5-8 Club is one of the two great traditional pillars of Jucy Lucys (cheese-stuffed hamburgers) in South Minneapolis. While Matt's is dark, dank, and seemingly unreconstructed after 50-plus years of service, the 5-8 Club has a clean, bright suburban sheen to it more evocative of a well-maintained Applebee's than a hole-in-the-wall tavern. Big portions, fried fare, and a neighborhood vibe make this a perfect gathering place for large groups looking for a casual meal at a convenient South Minneapolis eatery with some local flair. Beyond the obvious burgers, the onion straws of the 5-8 Club merit exploration—each order is huge in size, crispy in texture, and tasty in flavor. **Additional locations:** 2289 Minnehaha Ave. East, Maplewood, MN 55119; (651) 735-5858; 6251 Douglas Court North, Champlin, MN 55316; (763) 425-5858.

THE MINNESOTA STATE FAIR SURVIVAL GUIDE

Should you be fortunate enough to come to Minnesota during State Fair season, you must set aside half a day, at least, and attend. Should you come at some other time, you must consider seriously coming back to see the Fair.

Cumulative attendance regularly tops a million, and the **Minnesota State Fair** is to regular state fairs as the Death Star is to an asteroid. It teems with booths vending food and drinks; permanent buildings housing mind-blowing exhibitions of craft, kitsch, and art (the bizarrely topical and edgy seed art alone is worth the price of admission); and all manner of tertiary activity—politicians (up to and including the governor and US Senators) pitching their constituents; local food groups doing demonstrations; radio and television stations broadcasting; hog and horse judging; and so forth. It's a riotous carnival of life.

Many hundreds of fair food and drink items make the Fair one of the most interesting and sometimes terrific places to eat and drink in Minnesota. While much of what's available is old, boring garbage, or new, trendy garbage, much of the rest of it is surprisingly satisfying, stick-to-your ribs street food, or shockingly elegant, well-balanced fare that seems delightfully out of place.

The Basic Guidelines:

1. Unless otherwise directed or inspired, steer clear of thoroughly recognizable fair food. Pizza and hot dogs, for example, are widely available and mostly useless (the Blue Moon Drive-In's delightful sweet corn pizza is a notable exception).
2. The Agriculture building is a great place to frequent—past standouts have included a honey-sweetened lemonade and a rich, subtly flavored, local port wine ice cream.

3. The classic Fair experience is to obtain a large paper cone (or, if you're up for it, a straight-up plastic bucket) of freshly baked hot chocolate chip cookies from Sweet Martha's, and then walk over to the all-the-milk-you-can-drink-for-$1 booth and milk and cookie it up. This is highly recommended, in moderation. A cone of cookies can pleasingly sate four people, a bucket probably eight. Your stomach will inevitably be bigger than your eyes on this one.

4. Particularly if you're in from out of state, the real Wisconsin cheese curds of the Original Cheese Curds stand are worth the relatively brief wait in line. These hot little chunks of cheese are batter fried, and the light, crispy coating is a perfect complement to the lightly salted gooey cheese interior. Again, a little will go a long way—one order can make three or four people a lovely snack (see above).

5. The Summit Brewing company sets up a stage and booth near the International section of the Fair, and has become known in recent years for its Summit on a Stick, a wooden paddle with holes drilled into it, each hole holding a sample-size plastic cup filled with a different beer. The end result is roughly a pint of good local suds in a variety of styles. It's a particularly excellent move on a warm day. And Fair days overwhelmingly tend to be warm.

6. The Creative Activities tent has a sprawling collection housing the fruits of the annual canning and baking competitions. Gorgeous canned produce and jams stand adjacent to lit cases filled with cakes, pies, and local favorites such as *kransekake*, the traditional Scandinavian celebration cake made from stacked rings of pastry.

7. Any local food news source worth its salt (the *Star Tribune*, local news stations, various blogs) will have a pre-Fair roundup of new items. (The *Heavy Table*, heavytable.com, puts together a "wrecking crew" of 8 to 12 staffers who try 30 to 40 mostly new items on the first day of each Fair, making for the most comprehensive roundup of Fair food generally available.)

French Meadow Bakery & Cafe, 2610 Lyndale Ave. South, Minneapolis, MN 55408; (612) 870-7855; frenchmeadowcafe.com; Bakery; $$. Doing local and healthy food well before it was cool nationally (to say nothing of being cool locally), the pioneering French Meadow bakeshop proclaims itself the first certified organic bakery in the US. The cafe and restaurant is best known for its bread and breakfast, but it also offers a full-service dinner service. Its bread and dessert options feature yeast-free, vegan, sprouted grain, and Kosher Parve options, making it an ideal place to bring guests with special dietary requests, and while typically busy for breakfast, it's a pleasant, sunny, cheerful place to dine once you've finally staked out a table. The classic eggs Benedict is one of the best in the area.

Fuji Ya, 600 W. Lake St., Minneapolis, MN 55408; (612) 871-4055; fujiyasushi.com; Japanese; $$$. Fuji Ya has been serving Japanese food for more than 50 years, a good long time for any restaurant anywhere, and a jaw-dropping feat for a Midwestern place serving Asian food other than Chinese. (And heck, it's still a feat for a Chinese joint.) The secret to its success: good ingredients, a competent staff that handles the weekend rushes of trendy diners, and a sprawling menu that makes provisions for all types of appetites, from the curious to the conventional. Sushi is the mainstay, but diners can enjoy tempura, noodles, or sukiyaki, and the sake menu is worth reading if that's a drink you favor. **Additional location:** 465 Wabasha St. North, St. Paul, MN 55102; (651) 310-0111.

Gasthof zur Gemutlichkeit, 2300 University Ave. Northeast, Minneapolis, MN 55418; (612) 781-3860; gasthofzg.com; German; $$$. How serious can a restaurant be when two of its principal attractions are a giant glass boot full of beer and a miniature catapult brought from table to table to shoot snuff up the noses of its guests? How much does it matter that a restaurant be serious in the first place? If you're in the mood to drink, laugh, eat, and possibly dance and sing at the top of your lungs, the Gasthof is a pretty safe bet. Go with reservations, a big group, and a fearless attitude, and a good time is essentially assured. Go for a quiet German meal, and you're guaranteed to leave irritated at all the singing, dancing boors who ruin it for the rest of us. Combo platters offer a lot of assorted foods and are a great bet when you've got a big group. But if you're like most Gasthof denizens, you're not there for the food—you're passing a boot, admiring the waitstaff in their dirndls, and living it up, Northeast Minneapolis/college-student style. And, hopefully, being driven home by a designated nondrinker.

Hell's Kitchen, 80 9th St. South, Minneapolis, MN 55402; (612) 332-4700; hellskitcheninc.com; American; $$. Once a small, chef-driven, line-out-the-door downtown Minneapolis breakfast sensation, Hell's Kitchen has moved into a much grander space and become a breakfast institution. (Although the restaurant does serve lunch and dinner, it's known for its breakfast items, which are available all day.) Dozens of pajama-clad servers flood the multichambered, Ralph Steadman–themed (Hunter S. Thompson's visual wingman) subterranean space, which throbs with tourists on any given Sunday morning. The *mahnomin* wild rice porridge (featuring roasted hazelnuts, dried blueberries, and sweetened cranberries) is a favorite of Minnesota Senator Al Franken among others, and caramel-pecan rolls and lemon-ricotta hotcakes round out the list of local breakfast favorites. Rough-hewn, flavor-rich house-made peanut butter on black currant-and-coffee bison sausage bread is another specialty unique to the restaurant, which ranks among the most prominent breakfast joints in downtown Minneapolis. Though meat-laden, the bread is closer in flavor to a rich fruit bread, with the funky umami of the bison and black currants marrying beautifully with the peanut butter and/or jams available for spreading.

Holy Land Restaurant & Deli, 2513 Central Ave. Northeast, Minneapolis, MN 55418; (612) 781-2627; holylandbrand.com/restaurant.html; Middle Eastern; $$. A Twin Cities institution in the most expansive sense of the word, Holy Land is a specialty supermarket, a gyro-slinging food counter, a community center for recent immigrants, and general force for expanding Middle Eastern food—falafel, hummus, dolmades, and more—into the greater Minneapolis-St. Paul community. If you visit Holy Land's Central Avenue location when it's hopping with customers—as it often is—you'll be struck by how New York it feels. Service is brisk, and the crowd is a mix of all sorts of demographics—black, white, Middle Eastern, well-heeled, and working class, all queuing up for their daily fix of gyros or kebobs. A satellite location at the Midtown

Global Market also has both a supermarket and restaurant component, and adds to the general hubbub there and plays well with the Asian, Mexican, Scandinavian, and other cosmopolitan influences situated in the marketplace. **Additional location:** 920 E. Lake St., Minneapolis, MN 55407; (612) 870-6104.

Kramarczuk's East European Deli, 215 E. Hennepin Ave., Minneapolis, MN 55414; (612) 379-3018; kramarczuk.com; Deli; $$. Beyond its shelves of ethnic staples, baked goods, meat products, and condiments, this Ukrainian deli is the number one secret to a great cookout in Minneapolis—the deli's house-made bratwurst ranging from classic to currywurst to cherry bombs (spicy brats with dried cherries in them) are widely hailed as among the area's best. The brand is good enough that Kramarczuk's was able to break into the business of selling sausages at Twins games in Target Field, and the line to the deli's stand is typically one of the longest in the stadium. Kramarczuk's does most of its business over the counter, but there's also a cafeteria-like restaurant side to the business, too, where customers can order goulash, meatballs, pork chops, or meat-stuffed puffed pasties and enjoy them on the spot.

La Belle Vie, 510 Groveland Ave., Minneapolis, MN 55403; (612) 874-6440; labellevie.us; French; $$$$. Ask locals to name the best restaurant in the Cities, and luscious and luxurious La Belle Vie will often leap to their tongues—this highly polished French-inspired eatery combines sophisticated cuisine (think pan-roasted moulard duck breast with ricotta gnocchi or slow-poached sturgeon with

Minnesota Fish Fries

From deprivation comes celebration, or at least traditional celebratory foods—yesterday's poverty food or religiously restricted diet becomes today's proud badge of identity. Thus, the Upper Midwestern tradition of the fish fry, stemming from a Catholic observance of the 40 winter-spring days of Lent and meat-free Friday nights. There are few things more authentically Minnesotan than a Lenten Friday fish fry, and if you're seriously trying to get to know the culture (not just the young-people fancy-food culture, but the old- and middle-aged-people soul-food culture), there are few better opportunities.

On the traditional side of things, **St. Albert the Great**, a church in South Minneapolis, is known citywide for its bingo, bake sale, and fish fry celebration. One of the best-regarded from a culinary perspective, the food at St. Albert the Great is humble but prepared with care and real ingredients—it recalls a picnic lunch with family in the country, only served in a church basement to the

ramps) with highly polished professional service. Zagat and *Wine Spectactor* magazine have both recognized La Belle Vie for excellence, and Chef Tim McKee was the 2009 winner of the James Beard Award for best chef, Midwest. With the possible exception of **Manny's Steakhouse** (p. 32), no other area restaurant is so thoroughly synonymous with upscale dining—La Belle Vie has one of the best wine lists in the region (and possibly, the country), and its tasting menu is legendary and not for the faint-of-stomach. The accompaniment of a carnival-barker-like priest acting as the event's MC. (2836 33rd Ave. South, Minneapolis, MN 55406; 612-724-3643; saintalbertthegreat.org)

The **Red Stag's** year-round Friday fish fry is the upscale locavore haute cuisine–inspired spin on the rustic regional tradition, and more suited to newbies to the practice. In addition to cod, rockfish, and bluegill options with a sweet onion tartar sauce, smelt fries, crab salad, and seared scallops appear on the menu, elevating it a bit from a church basement affair. What's lost in community spirit and authenticity is gained in flavor and gastronomic precision and in the number of digits on the check. (509 1st Ave. Northeast, Minneapolis, MN 55413; 612-767-7766; redstagsupperclub.com)

restaurant's secret: Its lounge is surprisingly casual and reasonably priced, allowing for luxe bites and killer cocktails at a fraction of the price and pomp of the full-on dining experience. The cocktails are designed by local mixology maven Johnny Michaels and, by themselves, merit a visit to the restaurant.

Lions Tap Family Restaurant, 16180 Flying Cloud Dr., Eden Prairie, MN 55347; (952) 934-5299; lionstap.com; Burgers; $. A joyous, sometimes raucous ambiance, old-fashioned tavern decor, cheap prices, and big, greasy, juicy, back-to-basics and seriously tasty burgers (often tipped as best in the area) make this eatery a favorite of families from throughout the Western metro. While the fries are forgettable, the restaurant's picked up a rep for having 1919 root beer on draught, a Minnesota-made favorite. A caveat: The menu is as short as they come, so if you've got dietary restrictions, you're in for either a grilled cheese sandwich or a nonexistent meal while your friends happily mow down pounds of ground beef on buns.

Lord Fletcher's, 3746 Sunset Dr., Spring Park, MN 55384; (952) 471-8513; lordfletchers.com; Steak House; $$$$. Sometimes a restaurant is not merely a restaurant—it is also (or it is primarily) a "scene." Lord Fletcher's, located out in the western suburbs of Minneapolis, is one such restaurant. When summer rolls around, this sprawling multiple-level, indoor-outdoor becomes the hub of frolicking and gathering on the shore of Lake Minnetonka. Boats can (and do) pull right up to the restaurant's extensive patio, and diners can enjoy a host of old-school Middle American steak house favorites such as surf and turf, a classic Caesar salad, and Alaskan crab legs. At the end of the meal, you'll pay a fair price for both the ambiance and the well-prepared food, but if you've come on a glorious summer evening, you're unlikely to resent it.

Manny's Steakhouse, 825 Marquette Ave. South, Minneapolis, MN 55402; (612) 339-9900; mannyssteakhouse.com; Steak House; $$$$. Although the Minneapolis-St. Paul metropolitan area has a combined population of nearly three million people, Manny's cuts through the clutter and stands out as the signal "big deal" place to have dinner. The dry-aged steak is nationally reputable and impeccably prepared. One of the charms of the place is the "meat cart," a stainless steel wagon laden with plastic-wrapped cuts of meat that graphically illustrate the quality and mammoth size of the restaurant's main offerings. The servers are (to a man or woman) charmingly gruff, bluntly funny, and stunningly efficient. And the checks are enormous; if your party is able to walk out the door having spent less than $100 a plate, you've dodged some bullets. Bullets include good but mind-meltingly expensive seafood options, double-digit cocktails, and a wine list featuring bottles that wander up into the thousands of dollars. The atmosphere at Manny's errs on the side of being cacophonous, particularly if you're seated in the cattle-yard-esque main dining room, so if you're there to celebrate, be picky and demand a table in the bar section of the restaurant—they're worth the wait, unless you like yelling to be heard. Whether the ultimate price tag is worth it depends very much on your situation in life. For the businessfolk on expense accounts who are the restaurant's lifeblood, the atmosphere, quality of food, and style of service are a deal at half the price. For mere mortals, the choice is more complicated. Regardless, either bring a titanic appetite or an extra vehicle in which to cart home leftovers—each main can typically feed two hungry adults, and each side, probably four. One dessert split eight ways would still fill up everyone at the table. They're that big.

Matt's Bar, 3500 Cedar Ave. South, Minneapolis, MN 55407; (612) 722-7072; mattsbar.com; Burgers; $. No one knows how many hundreds of thousands (could it be millions? Sure!) of burgers have hit the perfectly seasoned grill at Matt's, but whatever the number, the place is a South Minneapolis institution. One of the birthplaces of the Jucy Lucy stuffed hamburger (along with the **5-8 Club,** p. 23, and Adrian's Tavern), Matt's has attracted far more than its share of local and national media attention on the strength of its dark, safely dangerous, charmingly old-school tavern interior and its humble burger-and-fries fare. The South Minneapolis soul food it dishes up is of debatable quality in terms of caliber of ingredients, but locals and visitors aren't coming to Matt's for world-class meat or fries, they're coming for history, for charm, and for an old-fashioned tavern burger with a Grain Belt Premium beer. And Matt's has all three in spades.

Mayslack's, 1428 4th St. Northeast, Minneapolis, MN 55413; (612) 789-9862; mayslacksbar.com; Pub; $$. Ask a Minneapolitan to name the number one sandwich that defines the city, and you'll hear a lot of answers: the Jucy Lucy hamburger, perhaps, or the Vietnamese *banh mi*, or maybe even the Mexican torta. But head to the Northeast part of the city and you'll more often than not hear "Mayslack's Garlic Roast Beef" as the answer of choice. This massive slab of a sandwich was originally created by a massive slab of a man, former pro wrestler and restaurant founder Stan

Myslajek, who started the bar/restaurant in 1955. The Mayslack's Original is a high stack of roast beef slow roasted in garlic for 8 hours and served with onions, banana peppers, coleslaw, and au jus, and it's a man-killer—it's worth paying the small split order fee and double teaming it with a friend. Live music and talkative locals make it a place worth visiting if you want to get a big garlicky taste of how it feels to live in "Nordeast."

Midtown Global Market, 920 E. Lake St., Minneapolis, MN 55407; (612) 872-4041; midtownglobalmarket.org; Varies; $–$$. As a more casual, ethnically diverse answer to San Francisco's Ferry Building or New York's Chelsea Market, Midtown Global Market is many things to many people. It's a cultural hub, filled with shoppers conversing in Somali, Arabic, Spanish, and English. It's a commercial kitchen (Kitchen in the Market), serving food cart vendors and other start-up food entrepreneurs. It's a day-to-day food market, selling fruits, vegetables, spices, olive oil, tortillas, and other staples to local families. It's an ethnic shopping mall, selling gifts, flowers and plants, arts, crafts, and more. And it's a veritable international smorgasbord, dishing up Scandinavian open-faced sandwiches (Cafe Finspang), chilaquiles (Sonora Grill and La Loma Tamales), Mexican tortas (Manny's), high-end cupcakes and other baked goods (Salty Tart), gyros (Holy Land), and burgers (Andy's Garage.) The Market regularly hosts festivals and other cultural events, including the excellent No Coast Craft-o-Rama, a holiday bazaar of locally Midwestern made arts and crafts that typically takes place in early December.

Milda's Cafe, 1720 Glenwood Ave., Minneapolis, MN 55405; (612) 377-9460; twincitiesfun.com/Mildas-Cafe-ID001460.html; American; $$. The homey, bustling, clean-cut melting pot that is Milda's is one of the less-than-heralded treasures in the Twin Cities. This profoundly unpretentious and popular diner in North Minneapolis does simple food well, and is one of the few places in the Cities where you can enjoy an honest-to-goodness weighty, flakey, soul-fulfilling Iron Range pasty (although only on Monday, Wednesday, and Friday, so plan accordingly). Breakfast is in the classic American "fill 'er up" tradition, but done with care and decent ingredients, so if you're in the neighborhood and wanting to start your day right, Milda's will get the job done.

Minneapolis Town Hall Brewery and Town Hall Tap, 1430 Washington Ave. South, Minneapolis, MN 55454; (612) 339-8696; townhallbrewery.com; Brewpub; $$. This nationally recognized, frequently award-winning brewpub has rapidly changing seasonal taps, an eye for creative beer concepts that tap into current craft brewing ideas without being irritatingly esoteric or trendy, and a small but nicely curated guest beer list that offers attractive options to visiting maniacs who, for unfathomable reasons, might not want to drink locally. Keep your food expectations low, and concentrate on the beer, which should be plenty to keep you distracted; **Chai's Thai** (p. 63) and the **Wienery** (p. 137) are near Town Hall

Brewery, and **Turtle Bread Co./Pizza Biga** (p. 135) are near Town Hall Tap, and should give you sufficient nourishment to help cushion the blow of a pint or three. Atmosphere in both locations tends toward the dark and noisy (particularly on weekends, which can be full-blown crowded), but the recently opened Tap is a little sleeker and more put together, while the original Brewery location is more of a bar bar. **Additional location:** 4810 Chicago Ave. South, Minneapolis, MN 55417; (612) 767-7307.

Murray's, 26 S. 6th St., Minneapolis, MN 55402; (612) 339-0909; murraysrestaurant.com; Steak House; $$$. Manny's. Murray's. It's easy to confuse the downtown's two most prominent steak houses if you've never been to either, but they're night and day. If **Manny's Steakhouse** (p. 32) is where well-off young bucks go to pound down $200 glasses of wine to help digest $90 slabs of meat, Murray's is a throwback to a more genteel era of dining. The atmosphere is dated with a vengeance, bedecked with mirrors, mid-20th-century architectural flourishes, and white tablecloths. An electric board of numbers is posted above the kitchen to signal to staff when a table's meal is ready. Cobb and Caesar salads share the menu with various cuts of meat, and the rich, balanced French onion soup has, the waiter might tell you, been on the menu every day for the past 65 years. The steak is well prepared and reasonably priced (particularly for lunch; the luncheon steak is a mere $20), and the blueberry pie is topped with fully flavored real whipped cream. The restaurant is self-consciously an eatery from the past, preserved in amber—if that's the sort of thing that intrigues you, neither the food nor the experience will disappoint.

Nye's Polonaise Room, 112 E. Hennepin Ave., Minneapolis, MN 55414; (612) 379-2021; nyespolonaise.com; Polish; $$$. Whether you love Nye's Polonaise Room or hate it—and there are locals who feel complicated, powerful mixes of both feelings when the place gets mentioned—you can't avoid it as a local institution. Named Best Bar in America by *GQ* in 2006, Nye's Polonaise combines a truly unforgettable interior design aesthetic with dueling pianos and one of the liveliest and longest-standing groups of regulars, bartenders, and servers to make for a remarkable scene. The bar/restaurant is really two places—the old bar called Nye's, and the (slightly) newer restaurant known as the Polonaise Room. Polka, Polish food, and a straight-outta-the-'50s supper club design sense that was come by honestly define this unique place, which in many ways is the living room of old "Nordeast" Minneapolis. Visitors will feel welcome

(many out-of-towners and young hipsters frequent either side of the establishment, and they're warmly tolerated) and most likely get a kick out of the scene. How could anyone (local or not) dislike the experience? Well, the food's expensive, the kitsch factor is astronomical, and the place is far from secret—cool kids can't score cool points by enjoying it ironically, so thoroughly is it celebrated. Well-known and celebrated as it may be, however, the sincere heart of Nye's still beats strongly, and those who come in with a song in their heart and an interest in old-school cocktails will leave happy.

Quang, 2719 Nicollet Ave., Minneapolis, MN 55408; (612) 870-4739; quangrestaurant.com; Vietnamese; $. Along with **Pho Tau Bay** (p. 110) and **Jasmine Deli** (p. 86), Quang is one of the hubs of the Eat Street Vietnamese food scene, serving a mixed clientele from all sorts of ethnic and economic backgrounds. Simple Vietnamese staples like *banh mi*, a bang-on pho with thinly sliced beef, and broken rice plates drive the trade at Quang, and the vermicelli noodle dishes are outstanding, if simple—it's worth keeping in mind that Quang is street food served up in a comfortably downmarket dining room that often teems with customers, not a reinvented Vietnamese bistro or fusion joint. If you want a similar experience with less chaos and line-waiting, go down the street to Pho Tau Bay; if you want to pick up a bunch of *banh mi* to go at an outrageously low price, Quang's your place.

Restaurant Alma, 528 University Ave. Southeast, Minneapolis, MN 55414; (612) 379-4909; restaurantalma.com; New American; $$$. Dine at the impeccably classy Restaurant Alma, and you'll quickly understand how Chef Alex Roberts won national recognition for his Midwestern cuisine—the menu is chockablock with elegantly balanced haute cuisine spins on local food, incorporating the likes of roasted rabbit, duck liver pate, and house-made sausage.

Seasonal, organic, and local are the watchwords, and the idiom is comfort meets high class. The wine list is diverse and lush to the point of being intimidating, but fortunately the service is anything but—Alma is a high-end place that puts an emphasis on serious but friendly service that gets the job done while making guests feel welcome.

Sea Salt Eatery, 4801 Minnehaha Ave., Minneapolis, MN 55417; (612) 721-8990; seasalteatery.com; Seafood; $$. Open from April through October, the open-air dining of Sea Salt Eatery at Minnehaha Falls is one of the great seasonal traditions of Minneapolis dining. Every summer, this park-shelter-style restaurant sprouts sprawling lines and amiable mobs of diners enjoying their pitchers of beer, peel-and-eat shrimp, fried fish tacos, seafood po'boys, and more at picnic tables with a view of the city's best-known waterfall and the scenic surrounding park. Sea Salt works with local standard-bearers Coastal Sea Food to obtain its fish, so quality is reliably high in an absolute sense—though affordable, the dishes at Sea Salt would stand up to the offerings at similar types of restaurants on either the East or West Coast. If you've got a group, go for the big "oil pan"—it's a collection of shrimp, oysters, pickled herring, and either a pitcher of beer or a bottle of house wine.

Sebastian Joe's, 1007 W. Franklin Ave., Minneapolis, MN 55408; (612) 870-0065; sebastianjoesicecream.com; Ice Cream Parlor; $. You can tell when a restaurant's hot by the wait for a table or the difficulty one faces in obtaining a reservation; you can tell when an ice cream parlor's hot by the length of line, and the good spirits with which people queue up and await their shot at the scoop or scoops of frozen glory of their choosing. By that metric, Sebastian Joe's has been quite hot for quite some time—this venerable (since 1984) ice cream parlor is rarely quiet, and on most summer nights the line stretches a consistent 20 or 30 people deep. Have no fear: it moves quickly, and some of the offerings available (like the shop's signature Pavarotti flavor, a dazzling banana, caramel, and chocolate chip blend that must rank among the cleverest frozen concoctions in the country) would be well worth twice the wait. The baseline is this: Sebastian Joe's makes rich, creamy, beautifully flavor-balanced ice cream, and if there's a better dessert out there, it's doing an awfully good job of hiding. **Additional location:** 4321 Upton Ave. South, Minneapolis, MN 55410; (612) 926-7916.

Shaw's Bar & Grill, 1528 University Ave. Northeast, Minneapolis, MN 55413; (612) 781-4405; shawsne.com; Burgers; $. If you're considering coming to the comfortable Northeast bar called Shaw's, particularly if you're from out of town and looking to explore the local food culture, there's one thing you need to know, and one thing only: the Shawburger. The description on the menu speaks for itself, describing a: "three-napkin burger, smothered with sautéed onions and mushrooms, Swiss and American cheeses, mayo, lettuce, tomato, bacon, and Shaw's signature sauce." Three napkins may be an understatement—this is a burger that can feed two adults, possibly three with the addition of fries. Frequent live bands and copious framed records and other such memorabilia give the bar a distinctly musical texture, and the animated conversations of committed regulars mean that you're steeped in Northeast culture from the moment you walk through the door.

Spoonriver, 750 S. 2nd St., Minneapolis, MN 55401; (612) 436-2236; spoonriver.com; New American; $$$. In tandem with old stalwarts like Lucia's and Birchwood and relative newcomers like Wise Acre and Corner Table, Spoonriver is one of the real drivers of the seasonal/local movement that has transformed Upper Midwestern dining in recent years. Chef-Owner Brenda Langton is a local fixture, and her ties to the local food movement extend fully through cookbooks and the Mill City Farmers Market out to the farms and ranches that dot the landscape of Minnesota and Wisconsin. Langton, active since opening her first restaurant in St. Paul in 1978, brings an interest in fresh produce and humanely raised meat that deeply informs Spoonriver's menu—guests can expect a civilized meal in a sleek, modern setting that is reflective of local food folkways and slow food ideals.

The Strip Club Meat & Fish, 378 Maria Ave., St. Paul, MN 55106; (651) 793-6247; domeats.com; Downtown St. Paul, 7th St. & Grand Ave.; Steak House; $$$. When young turks attack an old, established art form, watch out. That's the quick reduction of what's going on at The Strip Club Meat & Fish, a classic steak house concept reinvented by and for the young and/or gastronomically curious. Helmed by notable local Chef JD Fratzke and backer Tim

Niver (who opened the notable and now sadly shuttered Inn in downtown Minneapolis and Town Talk Diner in Longfellow), The Strip Club puts old favorites like grilled filet mignons and New York strips steaks side by side on a menu that features daily spins on Au Bon Canard *foie gras*, a "Poutine Obscene" of French fries, pork belly, white cheddar and port wine gravy, and a fried oyster po' boy. The bar is serious business, and whether you want to dive into vintage pre-Prohibition beverages or push forward into the future, The Strip Club's capable bartenders have you covered. For those willing to push into unfamiliar territory (there's not a lot of other contemporary joints sharing the Club's mostly residential St. Paul neighborhood of Dayton's Bluff), The Strip Club offers big rewards and a typically bustling, hipper-than-heck crowd that makes reservations a must.

Travail Kitchen & Amusements, 4154 W. Broadway, Robbinsdale, MN 55422; (763) 535-1131; travailkitchen.com; New American; $$. Travail was the "it" restaurant of 2011—a nod from *Bon Appétit* naming it the 4th "Best New Restaurant in America" sent an already raved-up spot into the stratosphere, turning wait times from glacially slow to insurmountable. (Multiple-hour waits have been known to happen at peak times—and no, they don't take reservations.) Why all the fuss? Travail runs on an absurdly absurd but fascinating premise: It's run by a rock-band-like collective of young chefs, with no executive chef. The food has a heavy molecular gastronomy influence (sometimes overly heavy; the foam doth flow with abandon at times). And the prices are astoundingly low for what you're being served. A beautifully executed and ridiculously entertaining liquid nitrogen "anti-griddle" dessert clocked in at around $5 on one visit, and an excellent and brobdingnagian charcuterie platter that could have fed three as a meal was a little less than $15. If you're going to go, keep in mind: Robbinsdale is a 20- to 30-minute trek from downtown Minneapolis. If you arrive later than 5 p.m., you may have to wait quite some time for a table. And the food, while copious in quantity and ambition, and sometimes quite brilliant, can range in quality. If you like a consistent experience and a sure bet, go elsewhere. If you're going to gamble, there may be no better place to throw the dice.

Vincent a Restaurant, 1100 Nicollet Mall, Minneapolis, MN 55403; (612) 630-1189; vincentarestaurant.com; French; $$$. Not every restaurant inspires love, but if you talk to customers of Vincent a Restaurant, that's a word you'll hear fairly frequently. What inspires their passion? It's something about the balance that Vincent strikes between upscale, proper, classically executed French food in its formal dining room and the raucously convivial atmosphere in its often stuffed-to-the-gills bar area. Vincent has a citywide reputation not just for its fine French classics but also for its burger, which features smoked gouda and braised short-rib meat stuffed inside seared ground sirloin. A satisfyingly pliable egg-bread bun is the perfect topper to the dish, which is one of the most distinguished local crave-worthy noshes in the city, sort of a high-concept twist on the Jucy Lucy that powers the South Minneapolis bar food scene.

Minneapolis Foodie Faves

Acadia Cafe, 329 Cedar Ave. South, Minneapolis, MN 55454; (612) 874-8702; acadiacafe.com; American; $$. A beautiful list of tap beers (a fairly good balance between high-class locals and famous national craft brewers) makes the Acadia Cafe a wonderful place to swing by for a pint or two and a long conversation and/or study break (presuming you're not one of those types who thinks that brew and knowledge are mutually exclusive). The space is light and airy, with tall ceilings and funky decor, and it lends itself well to midday meetings, powwows, and mid-afternoon escapes. The food is utilitarian, with an emphasis on straight-down-the-middle sandwiches and humanely grown, hormone- and antibiotic-free burgers.

Al Vento, 5001 34th Ave. South, Minneapolis, MN 55417; (612) 724-3009; alventorestaurant.com; Italian; $$. Al Vento strikes a rare balance between comfortable, fine dining–inspired atmosphere and menu with affordable neighborhood prices, making it a natural go-to for either a laid-back weekend chill-out sessions, or a fancy midweek splurge. The menu strikes a grand compromise between gourmet and grandma-friendly as well—while there are plenty of red-sauce-driven Italian-American classics to be had, there are also a number of more traditionally Italian options that tap into flavors like marinated olives, white beans, wild boar, and more. Without either fussing or slumming it, Al Vento does an admirable job of presenting Italian-American food in a neighborhood restaurant context.

Amazing Thailand, 3024 Hennepin Ave. South, Minneapolis, MN 55408; (612) 822-5588; amazingthailandusa.com; Thai; $$. Those in search of comfortably Americanized Thai food have a number of options in Uptown (Tum Rup Thai, Roat Osha, and so forth), but Amazing Thailand is one of the most reliable and certainly is the most beautifully decorated—the interior space features both a *tuk tuk* (an auto-rickshaw street taxi) and a strange but enchanting interior courtyard space with its own partial roof. Fried squid and Thai-style beef jerky with sweet chili sauce stand out among the appetizers, and the duck curry with pineapple is a pleasing standby. Located near **Kitchen Window** (great cookware shopping; see p. 8), **Dogwood Coffee** (a terrific post-dinner coffee; see p. 70), Magers and Quinn (a brilliant independent bookstore), and **Chino Latino** (post-dinner drinks; see p. 64), Amazing Thailand is a fine point on Hennepin Avenue at which to kick off an evening's carousing.

Amici Pizza and Bistro, 2851 Johnson St. Northeast, Minneapolis, MN 55418; (612) 781-5711; amiciusa.com; Pizza; $$. This profoundly snug neighborhood pizzeria in Northeast Minneapolis is lined with comfortable booths and classically styled tables and chairs. Oven-roasted chicken and other distractions like barley risotto and braised beef will only briefly distract the diner from the pizza section of the menu, which offers a small and focused selection of house favorites and a flexible build-your-own section featuring specialty ingredients like Capitola ham, a gluten-free crust option, and chipotle tomato sauce should please most comers. The pizzas tend to come out with thin, chewy, pleasingly crispy crust, a nice complement to the gourmet toppings that ride atop it in balanced proportions.

Anchor Fish & Chips, 302 13th Ave. Northeast, Minneapolis, MN 55413; (612) 676-1300; Irish; $$. When fish and chips are done right, as they are at Anchor Fish & Chips, the batter is rich but not overwhelming, and worn lightly by the fish—it's not a thick, heavy breading or greasy overcoat but rather a fluffy bathrobe of crispiness. Darkly lit but clean and modern with an open kitchen at the heart of the bar, the Anchor feels like a pub, and pints of beer and fish-and-chips are its stock in trade—its limited menu offers little else, although a few other items (the Helicopter Burger with a fried egg, Irish cheddar, and Fischer Farms ham for example) do pique the palate, and the toasty (a grilled sandwich with cheddar, ham, tomato, and onion) is a delight.

Aster Cafe, 125 SE Main St., Minneapolis, MN 55414; (612) 379-3138; aster-cafe.com; American; $$. Aster Cafe's casual space is a strange animal in the Minneapolis dining world—part cafe, part restaurant, part performance space, part bar, Aster sort of walks the line between any number of incarnations, performing well at all of them without being particularly outstanding in a particular direction. Tea-infused vodkas, rums, and tequila (such as pomegranate green tea vodka) make for some interesting drinking opportunities, and cheese or meat plates help groups of friends pass the time at Aster in a convivial and well-nourished manner. The atmosphere is clean and a bit minimalist, and it gets pleasantly shoulder-rubby when musicians take the stage . . . unless, of course, you weren't there for the live music. Call ahead. Aster serves late by local standards—until midnight, which is roughly equivalent to 4 a.m. on either of the coasts.

The Bachelor Farmer, 50 N. 2nd Ave., Minneapolis, MN 55401; (612) 206-3920; thebachelorfarmer.com; New Scandinavian; $$$. Although *The Golden Girls* have forever marked (tainted? blessed? crucified?) Minnesota as being the American extension of

Scandinavia, Scandinavian food is awfully difficult to find in this state's restaurants. For many Minnesotans, Scandinavian food is grandma food at best, poverty food at worst, but restaurant food . . . not so much. The closure of Aquavit in 2003 (and its subsequent success in New York City) was seen by many locals as a sign that fine-dining Scandinavian just couldn't succeed in the Cities, despite the area's concentration of wealth and diners of Scandinavian heritage. And then in 2011, along comes Bachelor Farmer. Opened by two of Minnesota Governor Mark Dayton's sons, Bachelor Farmer is an ambitious attempt to bring worldly, upscale Scandinavian fare to the Minneapolis Warehouse district. With its small plate menu, emphasis on bright, clean, simple flavors, and lovely interpretations of old standards like meatballs with lingonberry sauce, Bachelor Farmer is likely to impress and even startle those expecting food that is heavy or fussy. The attached Marvel Bar is fast becoming a presence on the Twin Cities craft cocktail scene, and diners should make sure to try at least one of Bachelor Farmer's "toasts"—lovely silver toast racks loaded with tiny, perfectly cooked slices of toast that serve as receptacles for goodies such as pates or cured fish.

The Bad Waitress Diner & Coffee Shop, 2 E. 26th St., Minneapolis, MN 55404; (612) 872-7575; thebadwaitress.com; Breakfast Cafe; $$. The Bad Waitress Diner & Coffee Shop has taken a risk in naming itself after a dispenser of lousy service, but the cheeky attitude has paid off—this is easily one of Minneapolis's most popular breakfast places, offering well-balanced and indulgent meals in a kitschy sci-fi/horror-influenced dining area. The name comes from the restaurant's procedure for ordering food: Guests fill out their own tickets at the table, bring them up to the counter, pay, and then return to their seats. The food is then brought to the table when it's  ready by perfectly competent and pleasant waitstaff. And while The Bad Waitress made its bones serving breakfast dishes such as a brilliantly balanced apple cinnamon french toast and a heartily delicious breakfast burrito, it's open until moderately late in the evening for those craving a satisfying Tex-Mex meal.

Bagu, 4741 Chicago Ave. South, Minneapolis, MN 55407; (612) 823-5254; bagusushi.com; Japanese and Thai; $$. Bagu is an affordable, low-intensity neighborhood sushi restaurant in a part of the city not lousy with them (which is to say Uptown, ground zero for the sushi craze in the Twin Cities). An outdoor patio makes for chilled-out dining opportunities in warmer weather, and the overall minimalist-but-cozy vibe makes it a fine low-impact choice for dining when you don't care to brave one of the A-list spots (**Origami**, p. 50; **Masu**, p. 96; **Fuji Ya**, p. 26). The chef's selection (or *omakase*) is done on a call-ahead basis, and is a nice way to take advantage of the fresher and/or more interesting cuts of fish available on any given evening. The availability of a Thai menu also makes it a more versatile choice for those with a mixed (i.e., sushiphiles + sushiphobes) party.

BANK Restaurant, 88 S. 6th St., Minneapolis, MN 55402; (612) 656-3255; bankmpls.com; American; $$$. If you can get past the soulless exterior of BANK, which is named for an institution of financial commerce and based on that hard-to-pin-down "modern American cuisine" ethic, there's a lot to love. The food is all about gentle twists on high-class business fare (marrow poutine, Scottish salmon with prosciutto and pesto, a "Cowboy Rib Eye" garnished with baked beans and spoon bread), and the dining room is plush, versatile, and civilized, boasting a private dining area, a wine vault, and a chef's counter. The overall feel can be seen as overstuffed and fussy or properly dignified—it depends on your mood and mission.

Bar La Grassa, 800 N. Washington Ave., Minneapolis, MN 55401; (612) 333-3837; barlagrassa.com; Italian; $$$. Instantly one of the hottest restaurants in town after it opened in 2009, Bar La Grassa has stayed busy ever since, sometimes with lines out the door on particularly hectic evenings. Helmed by the universally well-regarded Isaac Becker of 112 Eatery, Bar La Grassa's house specialty is fresh, house-made pasta, dressed with a variety of meats and sauces. Most nights, the dark, chic dining room crackles with electricity as patrons line up at the small bar or crowd tables, packing in delicacies such as soft eggs and lobster bruschetta, or cavatelli with braised rabbit. The restaurant was one of *Bon Appétit*'s 10 Best New Restaurants in America in 2010, Chef

Becker claimed the James Beard Award for Best Chef, Midwest in 2011, and in 2009 it took the *Star Tribune*'s "restaurant of the year" title. Minneapolis's paper of record called it an "adventure-in-the-making" and referred to its soft eggs and lobster as "heaven on toast"—a reasonably restrained description of a scrumptious dish.

Barbette, 1600 W. Lake St., Minneapolis, MN 55408; (612) 827-5710; barbette.com; French Bistro; $$. Barbette is the closest thing that the Twin Cities have to a Swiss army knife of restaurants—there's no more versatile place for a reliable, tasty meal any time of day for any reason. This French bistro–inspired eatery does a great breakfast/brunch; a charming soup- and sandwich-driven lunch service; afternoon coffee and bar snacks; happy hour; light, casual dinners; fancy, pricey dinners; late-night tapas and still more drinks. And it does them all 7 days a week. And while the place is known generally for its French bistro fare (mussels, croques madame and monsieur, a terrific steak tartare, seasonally influenced salads and specials), it's positively notorious for its thin, crispy, brutally addictive french fries. The dark, convivially bustling atmosphere is equally well suited to a first date or an after-work happy hour, and the art on the wall is often challenging and well-executed, and rotates regularly.

Barrio Tequila Bar and Cocina del Barrio, 925 Nicollet Mall, Minneapolis, MN 55402; (612) 333-9953; barriotequila.com; Mexican; $$$. Always reliable, lively, and popular, the relatively recently opened chain of Barrio restaurants takes Mexican street food to a high glossy polish and price accordingly. The Minneapolis and St. Paul locations in particular push an impressive and extensive list of specialty tequilas served with *compadres* (small side shots such as blood orange soda, apple ginger soda, or limeade) to cushion the blow or accentuate the effect. The *queso fundido* (melted cheese with poblano peppers) is a stick-to-the-ribs and satisfy-the-soul favorite, and Barrio offers larger plate entrees as well as perfectly respectable street-food-style tacos including *lengua* (tongue) and a fried mahimahi taco. There's even a gringo taco (hard shell, ground beef) for those in the mood. And, oh yes—the restaurant operates a food truck as well, so you may see them on the street during warm weather. **Additional locations:** 235 6th St. East, #100, St. Paul, MN 55101; (651) 222-3250; 5036 France Ave. South, Minneapolis, MN 55410; (952) 920-1860.

Be'Wiched Deli, 800 Washington Ave. North, # 101, Minneapolis, MN 55401; (612) 767-4330; bewicheddeli.com; Deli; $$. In contrast to the East Coast, Minneapolis-St. Paul has never had a rock-solid local sandwich and deli culture. Beyond burgers, which are present in numbers and strength, sandwich variety has been limited and quality questionable, outside of the ethnic options (Italian hot dagos, Vietnamese *banh mi*, and so forth). Therefore when Be'Wiched opened in 2007, it filled a void. Atmosphere is minimalist— this is a white-collar chow factory, albeit one dedicated to chef-driven, self-described "artisanal" sandwiches that use premium ingredients. The pastrami is respectable, the tuna is a tuna confit with black olive, cucumber, and preserved lemon, and even the egg salad is elevated with the addition of roasted peppers, both sweet and hot. While the street food boom will no doubt give Be'Wiched a run for its money, the variety and overall quality of its menu is a powerful draw.

Big Bowl Fresh Chinese, 3669 Galleria, Edina, MN 55435; (952) 928-7888; bigbowl.com; South Asian; $$. A local chain with restaurants scattered throughout the suburbs of Minneapolis, the classily fast casual Big Bowl concept is dedicated to serving up pan-Asian options with an emphasis on freshness and familiar flavors. While it lacks the gritty depth and eye-popping flavor of University or Nicollet Avenue Vietnamese dives, it has plenty of polish and serves up safe, approachable twists on Asian food that should please just about any crowd, no matter how diverse or inexperienced. The claypot curries pack a pleasing (if coconut-heavy) flavor punch, and diners should take care to try the restaurants' fresh, house-made ginger ale, which comes in varieties including passion fruit, green tea, and pomegranate. There's also a customizable stir-fry option for guests who want to mix and match from a list of sauce, protein, and rice/noodle options. There are numerous locations in the Cities, including the following. **Additional locations:** 12649 Wayzata Blvd., Minnetonka, MN 55305; (952) 797-9888; 1705 Hwy. 36 West, Roseville, MN 55113; (651) 636-7173.

Black Sheep Pizza, 600 Washington Ave. North, Minneapolis, MN 55401; (612) 342-2625; blacksheeppizza.com; Pizza; $$. It's understandable that the Upper Midwest is perceived as a pizza wasteland by New Yorkers, who live in a paradise where a decent slice is available at any given street corner. Black Sheep Pizza is doing its bit to turn that negative thinking around: Its anthracite coal–fired oven imparts a beautiful carbon-kissed crispness to the restaurant's thin-crust pizzas, and the ingredients are often sourced locally from farmers' markets, resulting in pizzas that taste fresh and wonderful. Founder Jordan Smith has a haute cuisine background that includes time cooking in Paris, Milan, the French Alps, and a Michelin-starred restaurant in London, and his experience shows in the balance of his pizzas and the quality of his ingredients. The salads are as good as anything else on the menu— start with the farmers' market special salad before you dig into your hot-from-the-800-degree-oven pizza. **Additional location:** 512 N. Robert St., St. Paul, MN 55102; (651) 227-4337.

Blackbird, 3800 Nicollet Ave., Minneapolis, MN 55409; (612) 823-4790; blackbirdmpls.com; Fusion; $$. The Minneapolis dining scene suffered a grievous blow in February 2010 when a fire led to the destruction of both **Heidi's** (p. 82) and Blackbird, two pillars of the local foodie community. But, happily, from the ashes of the fire came two renewed and reborn restaurants. Blackbird's reincarnation (on Eat Street rather than Southwest Minneapolis) meant more space for diners and a more welcoming and stylishly comfortable environment. The menu at this young-feeling spot is eclectic—Asian, French, Italian, and local food traditions all merge relatively seamlessly to create a surprising and often delightful mix of options for the curious diner. Local producers are often namechecked on the menu, and the restaurant's upscale take on the classic Vietnamese *banh mi* sandwich has a citywide reputation.

Blue Nile Ethiopian Restaurant, 2027 Franklin Ave. East, Minneapolis, MN 55404; (612) 338-3000; bluenilempls.com; Ethiopian; $$. Known more for its copious and well-curated beer selection than its serviceable and mildly seasoned Ethiopian food, Blue Nile is a gathering place for local hop heads (particularly members of the Surly Nation) and fans of its frequent live entertainment. The restaurant's eclectic, divey feel is just right for a rambunctious night on the town or a long, beer-fueled rap session, but not particularly well suited to fine dining. Bartender Al McCarty is well-known locally for his beer knowledge, and you can find his tasting notes online at thebitternib.blogspot.com.

Bradstreet Craftshouse, 601 1st Ave. North, Minneapolis, MN 55403; (612) 312-1821; bradSt.craftshouse.com; Craft Bar; $$. Located in the swanky Graves Hotel complex and named for decorative arts pioneer John Scott Bradstreet, Bradstreet Craftshouse features a menu of high-end ingredients turned out in comfort-food combinations (lamb sliders, fried oyster po'boys, lobster rolls) but it's best known for its classics-gone-modern craft cocktails—a mint julep built from Bulleit bourbon, demerara syrup, Peychaud's bitters, and mint, or a "Perfect Martinez" made from Hayman's Old Tom Gin, Dolin Sweet & Dry Vermouth, Luxardo maraschino cherries, and Fees orange bitters. Its upscale, urban atmosphere makes it a prime destination for a lively night on the town, but the high-end cocktails and glamorous setting come with a correspondingly upscale bill at the end of the evening.

Bread & Pickle, 4135 W. Lake Harriet Pkwy., Minneapolis, MN 55419; (612) 767-9009; breadandpickle.com; American; $$. The extensive encircling of Minneapolis lakes, rivers, and other waterways with parks, walking trails, bike paths, and other outdoor exercise amenities is a big fat blessing with just the tiniest hint of a curse—there are very few places to actually enjoy a good meal in the great outdoors that so typifies this city. Bread & Pickle is a nice move toward rectifying the oversight. Parked on the scenic shore of Lake Harriet and boasting a rustically comfortable outdoor seating area, Bread & Pickle brings a sustainable, locavore sensibility to summer park food, offering up the likes of an organic egg and cheddar breakfast sandwich, truffled popcorn, and frozen strawberry juice on a stick.

The Brothers Deli, 50 S. 6th St., Minneapolis, MN 55402; (612) 341-8007; thebrothersdeli.com; Deli; $$. The Brothers Deli is the closest one can get to New York City without boarding a

flight—even the line of this skyway-based delicatessen moves at a New York pace, snapping along smartly as customers efficiently rattle off their orders in a non-Midwestern fashion.

The restaurant can trace its history back to the 1930s, and there's a hallowed-by-time respect for ingredients that stands out amid a local sandwich shop culture that is sometimes lacking in grandeur. With credible corned beef and bagels and pastrami flown in from New York City, Brothers is one of the few local spots to nosh in East Coast fashion, and one of the best choices for diners eating within the labyrinthine and somewhat depressing Minneapolis skyway system. (That **Andrea Pizza** is one of the other standouts—and also happens to have a strong NYC vibe—is a pleasant coincidence; see p. 15)

Buca di Beppo, 1204 Harmon Place, Minneapolis, MN 55403; (612) 288-0138; Italian; $$. This burgeoning international chain (more than 80 restaurants in the United States and another 5 in the United Kingdom) got its start in 1993 with this location, in the basement level of a Minneapolis apartment building. Since then, it has boomed in popularity with a simple formula: huge, family-style portions, friendly service, kitschy decor, and bustling, musically laden atmosphere. Servings are mammoth and meant to be shared, and while you're not going to break any haute cuisine barriers, you're going to feed a large group a lot of red gravy soul food for a reasonable amount of money.

Buster's on 28th, 4204 28th Ave., Minneapolis, MN 55406; (612) 729-0911; busterson28th.com; Burgers and Beer; $$. Visitors seeking to partake in the exploding Minneapolis and St. Paul brew scene would be well advised to add Buster's on 28th to their list of must-try spots. An expansive beer menu (many dozens of bottles, about 30 taps and the occasional firkin of cask ale) lets visitors try taste after taste of local beer plus highlights from the national and international brewing scene. The "build your own beer flight" option is the choice of pros—five small glasses of craft beer appear on the table for a little more than $10, a perfect way to lay the groundwork for more serious drinking and sampling later on in the evening. The food is decent pub grub, including California-inspired pizzas and hearty burgers that are locally well regarded.

The Butcher Block, 308 E. Hennepin Ave., Minneapolis, MN 55414; (612) 455-1080; thebutcherblockrestaurant.com; Italian, $$. Don't let your initial best judgment keep you from entering and enjoying The Butcher Block—this restaurant is stuck with one of the worst locations in town, a windowless closet of a space in Northeast that was ultimately the death of Chef Don Saunders' much-lamented Fugaise. But once you make your way down the hallway and into the restaurant proper, it's a more pleasant experience—it's dark and cozy, and the straightforward Italian menu is comforting, simple, and competently executed. The *bucatini all' amatriciana* with *guanciale* and pecorino romano is as superb as it is classic. There's also a short (but well-curated) *grappa* list, if you'd like to finish your meal with a geographically appropriate *digestif.*

Butter Bakery Cafe, 3544 Grand Ave. South, Minneapolis, MN 55408; (612) 521-7401; butterbakerycafe.com; Bakery; $$. Independently owned and family-run, this neighborhood coffee-and-brunch spot is often crowded with locals jockeying for biscuits and gravy, omelets, and freshly (and competently) brewed cups of joe. Scoring a table or catching a server's eye can be a challenge, but the reasonably priced and well-executed food, scratch baked goods, thoughtfully prepared coffee, free Wi-Fi, and tolerably hip, casual atmosphere is a fine counterweight.

C&G's Smoking Barbecue, 4743 Nicollet Ave., Minneapolis, MN 55419; (612) 825-3400; (on Facebook); Barbecue; $$. This humble storefront was founded by Greg Alford, a Detroit native and 20-year veteran auto mechanic who had a passion for smoked meat. Wood-smoked ribs served dry or with sauce on the side are a sign of Alford's confidence level, and the restaurant is also known in the neighborhood for its range of sandwiches, including a house favorite Motor City corned beef served on a roll. Coneys (Michigan-style hot dog) are notably good here, too, if you're in the mood for a quick nosh. Equally crave-satisfying is the place's "loose-burger," a Detroit-inspired sloppy joe–like concoction served on a hot dog bun topped with mustard and onions. As is the case with many reputable 'cue joints, atmosphere is nonexistent, and while there are a couple of tables, C&Gs does an overwhelmingly successful carryout business.

Cafe Ena, 4601 Grand Ave. South, Minneapolis, MN 55419; (612) 824-4441; Latin Fusion; $$. Along with **Sonora Grill** (p. 126) and **Barrio** (p. 52), Cafe Ena represents the third-generation wave of Latin eateries—places that aren't catering to either recent immigrants or wide-eyed suburbanites, but rather to diners looking for a dash of culture-crossing flair. Influences from Venezuela to Argentina to Mexico to the Caribbean make Cafe Ena's menu a country-hopping adventure, and the chic but comfortable atmosphere is tailor made to put groups ranging in composition from tender lovers to awkward colleagues at ease. It's also kitty corner to **Patisserie 46** (p. 106), so if none of the desserts grabs your attention and it's early enough in the day, a quick walk across the street will yield good coffee and great pastry.

Cafe Levain, 4762 Chicago Ave., Minneapolis, MN 55407; (612) 823-7111; cafelevain.com; French; $$$. This quiet, intimate Nokomis neighborhood spot is thoughtfully tied to the land and seasons, and its short, focused menu changes with some frequency. Hearty country classics such as hanger steaks, liver pate, and roasted chicken bring French charm to the Midwest without straining too hard—there's nothing experimental at Levain, which is a great part of its charm. The theory appears to be that if mussels worked well with garlic, cream, butter, white wine, and a baguette 100 years ago, they'll probably work well today. It's a solid theory.

Cafe Maude, 5411 Penn Ave. South, Minneapolis, MN 55419; (612) 822-5411; Fusion; $$$. Small plates, dim lighting, and a killer drink menu make the classy, slightly off-kilter Cafe Maude a neighborhood favorite. Truffled fries, grilled flatbreads, and steak au poivre are the mainstays, as is a dessert composed of fresh baked chocolate chip cookies with vanilla bean milk. If you go, drink a black bunny for me—this crisp, refreshing blackberry mojito balances sweet berry flavor with the taste of tart lime and lifts everything up with gentle carbonation. Or savor one of Maude's "refreshments," carefully crafted nonalcoholic cocktails every bit as balanced and clever as their boozy colleagues.

Campiello Italian, 6411 City West Pkwy., Eden Prairie, MN 55344; (952) 941-6868; Italian; $$$. Once a staple of Uptown (a location that is now closed), Campiello seems to be getting by just fine in the 'burbs. Consistent service and a charming patio add value to a restaurant that prides itself on bulletproof, high-end interpretations of simple pasta dishes and wood-fired oven pizzas. Campiello is one of those rare restaurants that will bear multigenerational scrutiny—Grandma is as likely to enjoy it as a picky 13-year-old. The restaurant's excellent wine list and formidable cocktail menu (they're called "martinis," but once you start pouring black cherry bourbon or *tres leches* liqueur, you've strayed beyond the borders of Martiniland) make this place a no-brainer if you're in the neighborhood.

Cave Vin, 5555 Xerxes Ave. South, Minneapolis, MN 55410; (612) 922-0100; French; $$$. An intimate secret to those who frequent it, the long-standing but little written about Cave Vin is one of the hidden gems of Minneapolis, an unpretentious French bistro with a simple menu, civilized, romantic decor and atmosphere, and bold, clean, indulgent flavors. As the name implies, Cave Vin has a serious wine list, making it a fine spot for a second date or convivial meal with colleagues. Dishes are no more complicated than a pistachio pork tenderloin or frog legs sautéed with lemon, garlic, butter, and parsley, but they don't need to be—they're carefully prepared and served with love.

Chai's Thai Restaurant, 414½ Cedar Ave. South, Minneapolis, MN 55454; (612) 339-9385; Thai; chaisthai.com; $$. Chai's is one of those happy little gems of a restaurant that is easy to overlook but a pleasure to enjoy once you've found your way through the door. This tiny space contains a variety of Thai favorites that are convincingly flavorful with appropriate levels of heat and acid, served up by welcome-to-our-home-style service appropriate for a place slightly bigger than a typical suburban condo's dining room. Also worth knowing: If you like a drink with dinner, BYOB.

Chimborazo, 2851 Central Ave. Northeast, Minneapolis, MN 55418; (612) 788-1328; chimborazorestaurant.com; Ecuadorian; $$. Named for a volcano in Ecuador, this humble little restaurant in Northeast

Minneapolis is anything but a roaring natural disaster—it's a tidy, simple, welcoming place that serves food with profoundly balanced and delightful flavor profiles. From the soft, mild *llapingachos* (cheese-filled potato pancakes) to the vibrant *pescado encocado* (mahimahi in a rich coconut sauce with rice and sweet plantains), the menu surprises and delights without being in any way pretentious—it feels very "first generation" and uninterrupted. This isn't fusion food—it's Ecuadorian food, plain and simple. Textiles from Ecuador and traditional *quichua* music add to the experience.

ChinDian Cafe, 1500 East Hennepin Ave., Minneapolis, MN 55414; (612) 676-1818; chindiancafe.com; Chinese-Indian; $$. Born from the get-together of Nina Wong (born in Vietnam to Chinese parents) and Thomas Gnanapragasam (an ethnic Indian raised in Malaysia), ChinDian brings a whole lot of culinary history and firepower to the table with its boundary crossing, Asia-roaming fusion food. Wok noodles, Malaysian dishes like *nasi lemak* (fried chicken with coconut rice, a fried egg, and anchovies sambal), and Vietnamese noodle salads present diners with an appealing number of directions in which to travel while figuring out what to order. Atmosphere is casual—ChinDian is more of a place to nosh and hang out than a place to enjoy a full-on dining experience.

Chino Latino, 2916 Hennepin Ave., Minneapolis, MN 55408; (612) 824-7878; chinolatino.com; Fusion; $$. Uptown restaurant Chino Latino is famous—or notorious—for its frat boy humor billboard campaign (tuna taco jokes, anyone?) backed by restaurant group Parasole, one of the 800-pound gorillas of the local restaurant scene. This sprawling multilevel party den boasts an Asian/Latin inspiration (its mission is "street food from the hot zones"), and its dishes range all the way from discount-priced small plates during its multiple (and excellent) happy hours to massive, sharable entrees, topping out at a whole roast suckling pig that must be ordered in advance and should be shared with about a dozen friends. Sushi quality varies, but its sake list is excellent, and its mixed drinks are generally entertaining if not sophisticated. The big Latin-inspired platters (the plantain-based Nachos del Sol, for example) may be the most consistent value, but other entertainments (like Crack Ho Mojitos with real crack vials of customizable flavor or the brain-numbingly spicy Habañero Hell Poppers) are worth a try if you're in a festive mood. The restaurant's an acquired taste that some never acquire, but if you're aged 21 to 30—or just want to remember what that era felt like—it's a good place to scope out the Uptown scene. Tabs add up in a hurry, particularly when you're drinking, so keep your eye on your wallet.

Citizen Cafe, 2403 East 38th St., Minneapolis, MN 55406; (612) 729-1122; thecitizencafe.com; New American; $$. WPA-era vintage posters deck the walls and set the tone for Citizen Cafe, a thoughtful new neighborhood bistro with a mission to serve simple dishes made from good ingredients. The core of its offerings are comfort dishes like sandwiches (try the fried shrimp po'boy or house-made sausage of the day sandwich, in particular) or caringly crafted scrambles and hashes for breakfast. House-made cured salmon, carefully forged hollandaise sauce, and other thoughtful touches reflective of classic cookery make Citizen Cafe a happy balance between chef-driven passion and simple, accessible American food. And for a casual, affordable weekend brunch, it has few equals in the Twin Cities—there's a lot of bang for the buck and not too much to worry about amid its classy, Craftsman-style interior and professional service.

Cocoa & Fig, 651 Nicollet Mall, Minneapolis, MN 55402; (952) 540-4300; cocoaandfig.com; Bakery; $. Cake lollipops, French macarons, cupcakes, and Valrhona Chocolate Bouchons represent a mere fraction of the output of the newly established Cocoa & Fig bakery, the downtown Minneapolis representative of the new wave of high-end baked goods that has made Minneapolis-St. Paul a nirvana for sweets lovers. Run by partners Joe Lin and Laurie Pyle, the shop also does bake-to-order cakes and a catered gourmet s'mores service that brings together house-made graham crackers with three kinds of Ghirardelli chocolates and upscale marshmallows of various flavors.

Colossal Cafe, 1839 East 42nd St., Minneapolis, MN 55407; (612) 729-2377; colossalcafe.com; Breakfast; $$. The Colossal Cafe gained a recent spurt of fame via exposure on the Food Network's *Diners, Drive-Ins, and Dives* program—Guy Fieri was attracted to the place for its big, house-crafted classic breakfasts and its ironic name—the "colossal" space is absolutely tiny, seating only a few tables and a  small window counter full of guests elbow to elbow. Homemade buttermilk biscuits, big, fluffy, yeast-based flapjacks with real maple syrup, and a host of seasonal-vegetable-centered omelets make this a Middle American breakfast soul food choice. Be warned: Seating can be tough to come by during peak periods, and this is a cash-only restaurant. Colossal Cafe also makes take-home meals and seasonal pies, both of which tend to feature big flavor and generous portions.

Common Roots Cafe, 2558 Lyndale Ave. South, Minneapolis, MN 55405; (612) 871-2360; commonrootscafe.com; American; $$. Entrepreneur Danny Schwartzman's Common Roots Cafe may well be the most truly sustainable and determinedly local restaurant in the Twin Cities—concern for local purveyors and ecologically and socially sound practices drive every aspect of this business, which is a hugely popular destination for Uptown residents looking for a chilled-out place in which to breakfast, lunch, and study and/or work remotely. From a food perspective, it's known for its chewy, properly made bagels (possibly the best in the area, granting that it's a widely acknowledged bagel desert) and its addictive soft pretzels. The local beer selection is excellent, and seasonal influences make their presence felt on the constantly evolving menu.

Corner Table, 4257 Nicollet Ave., Minneapolis, MN 55409; (612) 823-0011; New American; $$$. Helmed originally by Owner Scott Pampuch (who has since gone on to a variety of other gigs, including hosting a national cable television food program and cooking at a country club), Corner Table has built a reputation as being one of the prime farm-to-table spots in the Cities. From foraged mushrooms to house-butchered cuts of heirloom pork, to seasonal veggies (in the summer) and pickled veggies (in the winter), the menu of Corner Table is a direct interpretation of the agricultural bounty that surrounds (and at times even pervades) the Twin Cities. With a warm, collegial atmosphere (it's not unusual to talk to your chef and eavesdrop on a forager or other such food-creating or gathering personality), eating at Corner Table is simultaneously a fine way to wind down and a good way to take stock of local food culture—geographically, seasonally, and otherwise. Anything pork (particularly pork belly) is likely to be stellar, and house-made sodas and pickled sides add interest to any meal.

Craftsman, 4300 E. Lake St., Minneapolis, MN 55406; (612) 722-0175; craftsmanrestaurant.com; New American; $$$. For a number of years, the Craftsman was one of the leading lights of the seasonal local dining scene, its gorgeously tasteful hardwood interior playing host to the regionally famous charcuterie plates of Chef Mike Phillips, house-pickled sides and appetizers, and seasonally driven menus that included a serious craft cocktail component. The departure of Phillips (who now heads up the Three Sons Meat Co.) left the Craftsman in a temporary spin, but the restaurant is back on track and serving up finely realized dishes informed by local purveyors and a strong sense of seasonality. Those looking for a tasteful Minnesota- and Wisconsin-centered meal amid decorative jars of pickled local produce need look no farther. And if it happens to be warm outside, the patio is one of the city's most charming.

Crave Restaurant, 1603 West End Blvd., St. Louis Park, MN 55416; (952) 933-6500; craveamerica.com; Fusion; $$$. If you're doing a swanky business lunch in the western suburbs, 50/50 odds it'll be at one of the numerous locations of Crave Restaurant. From sushi, to wings, to fondue, to kogi beef tacos, to sliders, to steaks, to ahi tuna, to gourmet pizza, the restaurant covers just about every high-end comfort base except for caviar and blini. The food tends to be consistently competent, as does the service, and the atmosphere is cool, chic, and well put together, much like the clientele. **Additional locations:** 368 South Ave., Bloomington, MN 55425; (952) 854-5000 (Mall of America); 825 Hennepin Ave., Minneapolis, MN 55402; (612) 332-1133; 3520 W. 70th St., Edina, MN 55435; (952) 697-6000.

Curran's, 4201 Nicollet Ave., Minneapolis, MN 55409; (612) 822-5327; currans-restaurant.com; American; $$. The beauty of old warhorse restaurant Curran's (in business since 1948) is its unpretentious simplicity. If you've ever wanted to go to Perkin's—but with food made from ingredients, rather than cans—Curran's is the place, right down to the ambitious selection of house-made pies. The most modern thing on the menu is probably the taco salad—otherwise, it may as well be 1983, with a preponderance of respectably prepared Middle American chow including burgers, monte cristo sandwiches, barbecue ribs, and meat loaf. Settle into a booth, order a coffee, and relax, you've traveled back in time.

Dogwood Coffee, 3001 Hennepin Ave., Minneapolis, MN 55408; (612) 354-2952; dogwoodcoffee.com; Coffee; $$. Dogwood Coffee describes itself as a "small, quality-focused roaster," and its dedication to high-end single-cup coffee brewing puts this spartan little java bar on the forefront of third wave coffee in the Twin Cities. With public cuppings on the first and third Thursday of every month, a preposterously luxe and expensive Clover machine for making coffee, and single-origin coffees prepared to order, Dogwood caters to coffee-drinking professionals: gourmets, fellow baristas, and caffeine addicts with a lust for flavor. It also serves pastries from **Rustica** (p. 119).

Dong Yang Oriental Foods, 735 45th Ave. Northeast, Hiltop, MN 55421; (763) 571-2009; Korean; $$. Keep driving for long enough on Central Avenue in Northeast Minneapolis, and the neighborhood gets real ethnic and real interesting in a hurry—Dong Yang, a Korean grocery and lunch counter, is just one of a number of intriguing Asian, Middle Eastern, or Indian establishments in this working-class cosmopolitan district of Minneapolis. This crammed-to-the-ceiling Korean grocery store is extensively stocked with the kind of specialty foods (including sauces, spices, stocks, and other power ingredients) you'll want before tackling Asian recipes in general and Korean recipes particularly. But if you walk far enough into the store and turn left, you'll discover Dong Yang's secret: a little room with four small tables and a counter where you can eat Korean food on-site. The burn-your-hands-off-on-the-stone-bowl *bibimbap* is where it's at—in cold weather, it's a delight to eat the hot crispy rice that collects where the rice hits the rock, everything rich in flavor from the ingredients (marinated beef and an egg, for example) sitting above it. Dishes generally come with a nice collection of cold, sometimes spicy, generally pickled sides, almost always including kimchi.

duplex, 2516 Hennepin Ave. South, Minneapolis, MN 55408; (612) 381-0700; duplexmpls.com; Bistro; $$. Uptown's duplex restaurant (not capitalized, in the interest of scoring coolness points) is one part hip Uptown bistro, one part comfort-food-dispensing burger joint, and one part, well, actual residential duplex that was converted into a restaurant. Locally famous for its anything-but-light poutine (a Canadian dish featuring fries topped with melted cheese curds and brown gravy), duplex also offers a serious bacon burger, pasta options, and a vegan hummus wrap. Its funky, cozy atmosphere got it named best restaurant for a first date by alt weekly *City Pages*— more than one critic has described the space as "intimate."

Ecopolitan, 2409 Lyndale Ave. South, Minneapolis, MN 55405; (612) 874-7336; ecopolitan.com; Vegan; $$. If the name "Ecopolitan" sounds to you less like a restaurant and more like a fringe lifestyle, you're on the right track—its oxygen bar, emphasis on organic vegan raw food, and use of "un-cooking" techniques make it one of the most unusual places to eat in the Twin Cities, albeit one with a devoted following. Salads are a given, but the place gets most interesting when it emulates traditional dining choices within its own idiom: witness the breakfast "Rawmlette," which is "two banana-coconut-flaxseed 'omelette' shells with macadamia-cashew 'cheese,' avocado, carrot, onion, and cilantro" or any of the house pizzas, which are buckwheat-herb "crusts" spread with assorted vegetables and "sauces" such as hummus, olive tapenade, or pine nut pesto. The quality of ingredients is good, but an open mind and/or a long-standing devotion to raw food will help a newcomer appreciate the Ecopolitan's unique charms. And if all else fails, there's a heck of a good smoothie menu.

El Meson, 3450 Lyndale Ave. South, Minneapolis, MN 55408; (612) 822-8062; elmesonbistro.net; Spanish; $$. Warm, dimly lit, and rustic, El Meson does a lively local interpretation of a Spanish gastropub, serving simple Spanish and Caribbean food that soothes and pleases. Owner Hector Ruiz (who presides over the somewhat more chic and forward-looking **Cafe Ena;** p. 61) has put together a comfortable space that does as fine a ceviche as is known in the Twin Cities, a small, well-edited selection of classic tapas, Spanish/

Caribbean entrees, and a reliably tasty sangria served by the glass or carafe. As might be expected, the lunch buffet disappoints compared to a full-service dinner experience. Weekend live flamenco performances fill the room with sound and color.

El Nuevo Rodeo Restaurante y Dance Club, 2709 E. Lake St., Minneapolis, MN 55406; (612) 728-0101; elnuevorodeo.com; Mexican; $. You probably didn't come to Minneapolis for its Latin club scene, but it's here, and it's serious business—come to El Nuevo Rodeo on a Friday or Saturday night, and a crowd of impeccably (and flamboyantly) dressed patrons queue up, ready to dance all night to tribal techno or norteño hits. The food is simple and soulful, ranging from *flautas* to table-side guacamole to cactus salad to Aztec tortilla soup to classics like tacos (corn or flour tortillas), tamales, and sizzling fajitas. And if you're in the mood to explore and get dangerous, the red-hot pineapple chipotle margarita dangles on the drinks menu, exuding an aura of temptation and menace.

El Taco Riendo, 2416 Central Ave., Minneapolis, MN 55418-3712; (612) 781-3000; eltaco-riendo.com; Mexican; $. Depending upon whom you talk to, the name of El Taco Riendo means the laughing taco (*riendo*) or the running taco (*corriendo*), and both are suggestive of a practical joke. The food here is serious, though, and since opening in 2009, it has arguably become one of the go-to taquerias in Minneapolis and certainly one of the go-to taquerias in Northeast. Tacos are obviously the big draw, and the tender, rich *lengua* (beef tongue) tacos are some of the favorites of the house. Asada, barbacoa, and carnitas are just a few of the other choices available on the extensive list of options, which are fairly traditional Mexican variants—no cute fusion Thai tacos or sushi tacos here.

Element Wood Fire Pizza, 96 Broadway St. Northeast, Minneapolis, MN 55413; (612) 379-3028; elementpizza.com; Pizza; $$. Element comes amid a spate of recent wood-fired pizza places to open in the Twin Cities, and it brings it with the best of them, serving up simply conceived but artfully executed pizzas with straightforward names like "Water," "Fire," "Farmers," "Old World," and "Terra." The marble-clad oven is a beauty, and it turns out pizza with chewy/crispy/slightly charred crust likely to please even dedicated pizza fans. The space is warm and cozy to the point of getting crowded in a hurry, but once you're seated, food tends to come to you fast—that's the beauty of a hot oven.

Emily's Lebanese Deli, 641 University Ave. Northeast, Minneapolis, MN 55413; (612) 379-4069; emilyslebanesedeli.com; Middle Eastern; $$. This tiny little grocery store/two-table deli is less a hole in the wall than a pinhole in the wall, but Middle Eastern food fans swear by its product, which tastes fresh, lively, and made with real love. In business for more than 35 years, Emily's serves up a simple menu (hummus, *baba ghanoush*, fried kibbi sandwiches) and does some of the best stuffed grape leaves in the area.

Filfillah Market and Restaurant, 4301 Central Ave., Columbia Heights, MN 55421; (763) 781-2222; filfillah.net; Turkish; $. Two words that rarely go together are "gyro plate" and "fresh," but there you have it—the Turkish restaurant and Middle Eastern market known as Filfillah makes its schwarma daily, and it's lively, rich, flavorful, and tender, accompanied by house-made bread and veggies that taste surprisingly vibrant considering the normal gyro/schwarma standard in this town. A somewhat cavernous feeling and oddly shaped wood-clad dining room bracketed with booths puts this place somewhere between a fast-food restaurant and a typical ethnic eatery, so don't go for atmosphere—go for the house-made baklava, which is super crispy, beautifully spiced, and vibrantly honeyed but not dripping in honey or disgustingly oversweet, as is so often the case.

First Course Bistro, 5607 Chicago Ave., Minneapolis, MN 55417; (612) 825-6900; firstcoursebistro.com; New American; $$$. As its name implies, First Course is a cozy, classy neighborhood place that offers small plates and moodily romantic ambiance. Spanish flavors (olives, cured pork, manchego cheese) mingle freely with pastas, seared tuna dishes, and more substantial entrees driven by high-end proteins accented with carefully prepared sauces and chutneys.

Fogo de Chao Churrascaria, 645 Hennepin Ave., Minneapolis, MN 55403; (612) 338-1344; fogodechao.com; Brazilian Steak House; $$$. Brazilian *rodizio* (rotisserie grill) isn't a style of cooking and eating with much presence in Minneapolis (or the Upper Midwest in general, for that matter). But Fogo de Chao, an international

Brazilian steak house chain, saw an opportunity to bring its exotic-meets-upscale comfort food formula to the Twin Cities, and it caught on quickly. The concept is simple: An infinite series of chefs bring skewers of freshly grilled steak, sausages, or pork to the table; guests indicate how much meat they'd like sawed off the skewer, and the process repeats until the meat is triumphant. Fogo de Chao is expensive but the quality is consistently high, and the luxe atmosphere makes it a good fit for business meetings, particularly when a corporate entity is footing the bill. And despite Fogo's meat-forward image, the salad bar is worth checking out—it's massive and beautifully stocked.

Galactic Pizza, 2917 Lyndale Ave. South, Minneapolis, MN 55408; (612) 824-9100; galacticpizza.com; Pizza; $$. At least 50 percent of Galactic Pizza's notoriety stems from the fact that it's delivered by a superhero-costumed delivery dude driving a tiny, brightly colored car. As exciting as this point may be, it misses the heart of the matter, which is that this Uptown institution makes a damned good pizza pie. Fresh, organic ingredients and novel combinations (the Paul Bunyan features wild rice, mozzarella, bison, and tomatoes sourced locally) mark Galactic's product as one of the most unusual in the market, and one that creates fans and converts where other pizza places merely have customers.

Gandhi Mahal, 3009 27th Ave. South, Minneapolis, MN 55406; (612) 729-5222; gandhimahal.com; Indian; $$. Gandhi Mahal's richly sauced, deeply spiced Mughal-style entrees supply locals with a commodity that is in scarce supply: Indian food with luxurious depth and mouthfeel. In contrast to some of the more austere southern Indian food that is predominant in the area, Gandhi Mahal's rich entrees and various flavored naans give diners an indulgent experience that is nice complemented by the cozy, knickknack- and art-driven atmosphere of the restaurant's sizable dining room. A recent expansion provided Gandhi Mahal with a community and events space, and avid fans of local dining will be pleased to note the restaurant's use of local produce and proteins. As an added bonus, a variety of yogurt-based lassi drinks that go far beyond the standard mango choice offers a buffet of options for the non-drinker.

Gardens of Salonica New Greek Cafe & Deli, 19 5th St. Northeast, Minneapolis, MN 55413; (612) 378-0611; gardensof salonica.com; Greek; $$$. Twenty years of consistently fine Greek food have allowed the Gardens of Salonica to grow into a local institution, anchored by its cuisine and enriched by community events such as its knowledge-and-grub Symposia series and holiday visits from Santa Claus. Local and seasonal offerings go far beyond the usual Greek diner fare; a lamb-baked-in-parchment dish called *kleftiko*, for example, is described by the restaurant as follows: "It means 'stolen' because the 'Kleftes' or guerrillas of the Greek War for Independence (1820s) 'raided and confiscated' livestock from their enemies to feed their troops. In order to escape detection by telltale smoke signaling their position, the Kleftes buried meat and vegetables in fire pits and covered them with dirt, leaving them to cook in their own juices. At the Gardens we re-create this tradition by parceling braised lamb shoulder in parchment with eggplant, red bell peppers, fava beans, feta, and fresh savory herbs. Then we bake the tied-up packets until the flavors mingle into a singular dining experience you must not miss." If you're a nut for Mediterranean gastronomy and/or history, you've found your place.

Gather at the Walker, 1750 Hennepin Ave., Minneapolis, MN 55403; (612) 253-3410; info.walkerart.org/visit/dining.wac; American Bistro; $$$. An ambitious culinary program and a dazzling view make Gather (the restaurant at the Walker Art Center) one of the most intriguing restaurant spaces in Minneapolis. A labyrinth-like parking garage and difficult-to-navigate museum interior also make it one of the least accessible, which at least partially led to the demise of its predecessor, the Wolfgang Puck–run 20.21. Still, if you can find your way there, there are rewards to be had: the food is upscale but not fussy, with profoundly comforting elements. At the time of its debut, it featured a grilled cheese made with Prairie Breeze cheddar from Milton Creamery in Iowa, one of the many rising star cheeses in the Minnesota/Wisconsin/Iowa cheese belt—while rich and luxurious, it was also simple and familiar, qualities that often get lost in the shuffle of high-end dining.

Ginger Hop, 201 East Hennepin Ave., Minneapolis, MN 55414; (612) 746-0305; gingerhop.com; Asian; $$. Jaw-dropping moving fan sculptures line the ceiling of Ginger Hop's bar, making an entrance to this chic pan-Asian eatery ("East Meets Northeast") a memorable one. The menu jumps around pleasantly, stopping in Thailand (sweet-meets-spicy curries), China-by-way-of-San Francisco (stir-fries and fried rice), Brooklyn and/or Korea (a Reuben jazzed up with kimchi and Sriracha mayo) and the UK-via-Minnesota (fish and chips made from a walleye fillet and served with wasabi tartar sauce). Asian purists and chow hunters may find their food bland and safe; more relaxed or uninitiated palates are likely to relax and enjoy. Plenty of vegetarian options and some nice hard-to-find beer choices broaden the appeal, and the house cocktail menu is clever and pleasing, if a bit on the sweet side. Ambiance is eye-pleasing and soothing, with plenty of space to spread out and relax, which can be a challenge in some of Northeast's smaller and trendier destinations.

Good Earth Restaurant, In the Galleria, 3460 W. 70th St., Edina, MN 55435; (952) 925-1001; goodearthmn.com; Fusion; $$. Though part of Parasole, one of the area's biggest restaurant groups, both Good Earth locations reach out to eaters sometimes suspicious of heavily processed, artery-punishing "corporate food" by offering a menu driven by organic, vegetarian, and health-conscious items. Spurning hippie disarray for a sleek, prosperous California vibe, Good Earth doles out edamame, tropical salads, light sandwiches and wraps, and other such fare to suburban ladies who lunch. **Additional Location:** 1901 Hwy. 36 W, Roseville, MN 55113; (651) 636-0956.

Gorkha Palace, 23 4th St. Northeast, Minneapolis, MN 55414; (612) 886-3451; gorkhapalace.com; Nepali-Indian; $$. Carefully balanced flavor profiles and a subtle use of spice make the Indian-Tibetan-Nepali restaurant Gorkha Palace one of the top choices for visitors seeking out something from the Indian subcontinent while in the Twin Cities. *Momo* (steamed dumplings filled with vegetables, optional protein choice, and spices, served with tomato chutney) is a house specialty, the yak *momo* doubly so. If novelty gets you through the door, so much the better—reliably warm service and bright, splashy flavors powered by as much local produce as the seasons allow make it a place you'll be likely to revisit. And while you're eating, check the Himalayan-themed wall mural, which enchants with its romantic simplicity.

Grand Cafe, 3804 Grand Ave. South, Minneapolis, MN 55416; (612) 822-8260; grandcafempls.com; New American; $$. This sleek bistro presents a simple menu driven by local produce and meat (Wild Acres chicken, Au Bon Canard duck, and so forth) in a way that evokes the small eateries of Europe, which seem to effortlessly weave the agricultural bounty of their region through their dishes. Seasonal changes to the menu are typical, and Grand Cafe goes out of its way to make use of pickled and otherwise preserved local food when seasonally appropriate, i.e., throughout the 4- to 5-month annual hazing we call "winter." A well-curated wine menu is a nice complement to the carefully honed choice of food, and makes, overall, for a supremely civilized dining experience.

Grumpy's Bar & Grill, 1111 Washington Ave. South, Minneapolis, MN 55415; (612) 340-9738; grumpys-bar.com; Pub; $$. Those seeking to drink (and boogie) like a local are advised to try Grumpy's, particularly the somewhat rough-and-tumble but still welcoming Northeast location. Great jukeboxes and cold beer anchor the brand. Downtown and Roseville locations offer restaurant menus focused on fried cheese and/or meat-related items ranging from mini corndogs to all manner of burgers; Northeast is strictly peanuts and frozen pizzas, although Friday afternoons will sometimes feature an impromptu feast put on with whatever the manager feels like cooking up. **Additional locations:** 2200 4th St. Northeast, Minneapolis, MN 55418; (612) 789-7429; 2801 Snelling Ave. North, Roseville, MN 55113; (651) 379-1180.

Haute Dish, 119 Washington Ave. North, Minneapolis, MN 55401; (612) 338-8484; haute-dish.com; American; $$. Chef Landon Schoenefeld has a local reputation as the bad boy of good eats, having bounced from restaurant to restaurant in a blaze of drama and well-reviewed food. Finally landing at his own spot in 2010, Schoenefeld has blossomed as a chef, taking familiar Midwestern favorites (like the "hotdish" casserole that gives the place its name) and turning them on their heads. From General Tso's sweetbreads with *foie* fried rice to a Tater Tot HauteDish with short ribs and porcini bechamel, Schoenefeld goes big and bold with his flavors, proteins, and sauces. The bar is one of the best in downtown Minneapolis, offering a small but nicely executed collection of favorite cocktails including the best mint julep you've probably ever tasted—it puts good bourbon (Woodford Reserve) first, and lets mint, soda, and a bit of simple syrup play supporting roles. Along with **The Bachelor Farmer** (p. 48) and St. Paul's **Heartland** (p. 148), Haute Dish may be one of the quickest ways to give visitors a chance to taste local flavor in a fine dining setting, even if Haute Dish's chic and often late-night scene defies some white-tablecloth conventions.

Heidi's Minneapolis, 2903 Lyndale Ave. South, Minneapolis, MN 55408; (612) 354-3512; heidismpls.com; New American; $$$. Artful plating, sophisticated ingredients, high-concept food, and a special "Shefzilla Surprise" option that leaves diners in the dark until the food hits the table make Heidi's one of the prime fine dining destinations in Uptown, a restaurant-dense district rich with competition. Chef Stewart Woodman's outsize personality burns up the Internet on his Shefzilla blog, and he manages to harness a fair bit of that fire to turn out classically informed, luxe, and often molecular gastronomy-based dishes that will please the most cosmopolitan of guests. The atmosphere feels as modern as the food—the chic, dimly lit space is anchored by a tree-like sculpture and offers a prominent view of the kitchen.

The Herkimer Pub & Brewery, 2922 S. Lyndale Ave., Minneapolis, MN 55408; (612) 821-0101; theherkimer.com; Brewpub; $$. Brewpubs are an increasingly common sight in the Twin Cities and surrounding communities, but The Herkimer takes an interesting approach to the genre—all its beers are directly

German inspired, without any of the Belgian or American flights of whimsy that so typify the modern gonzo homebrewing ethic. The result is clean-tasting, refreshing, classic beers that will make purists proud to put the pint to their lips. The atmosphere is as crisp and neat as the brew—everything's clean and polished, light-colored lacquered wood predominates, and the in-house shuffleboard games are works of modern art. The Herkimer is also a Packer bar (notoriously so, since Minneapolis-St. Paul is Vikings country), so if you're inclined to root for the Green and Gold on game day, this is one place where the game will always be on and the fans will be on your side.

Himalayan Restaurant, 2401 E. Franklin Ave., Minneapolis, MN 55406; (612) 332-0880; himalayanmomo.com; Nepalese; $$. This comfortable neighborhood Nepalese restaurant serves up its famous *momos* (dumplings) in two standard varieties: conventional chicken, and the earthier yak variety. Dishes come with brightly herbed sides and sauces, and rice, lentils, and dried fruit help keep the meals relatively balanced and healthy. While an appealing dinner destination for those looking for exotic fare, the Himalayan also does a fine business at lunch—its buffet provides a nice sampling of its more accessible fare for a low price.

Hoang Thien Y Deli, 2738 Nicollet Ave. South, Minneapolis, MN 55408; (612) 874-9145; Vietnamese, $. Restaurants don't come much smaller or much grittier than Hoang Thien Y, a Vietnamese restaurant on Eat Street catering to first-generation immigrants and serving simple, hearty, deeply flavorful food evocative directly of the old country. Atmosphere is spartan at best, but the prices are low and the surprise factor high—wander too far into the difficult-to-parse menu and you could stumble upon something wonderful and new, or something laden with tripe. Most dishes come in pieces and are assembled by the diner to suit their own palates, which makes the experience that much more challenging and/or entertaining; step up to the brightly colored and somewhat daunting desserts to finish the meal. Chowhounds with a love of adventure should make sure to add it to their peregrinations along and around Nicollet Avenue.

Hong Kong Noodle, 901 Washington Ave. Southeast, Minneapolis, MN 55414; (612) 379-9472; mnhongkongnoodle.com; Chinese; $$. Even an absurdly huge menu (even by Chinese-American restaurant standards) can't disguise the pleasure of Hong Kong Noodle, a campus restaurant typically filled with a pleasing 50/50 mix of white-bread Midwesterners and native Chinese language speakers in search of familiar flavors. Big plates of food, fresh-tasting vegetables, lip-smackingly tasty noodles, and the constant temptation to dive still further into the absurd encyclopedia of a menu are all convincing reasons to give Hong Kong Noodle a try, or come back for more.

In Season, 5416 Penn Ave. South, Minneapolis, MN 55419; (612) 926-0105; inseasonrestaurant.com; New American; $$$. In Season is a chef-driven, French-inspired new American eatery headed by Chef Don Saunders. Saunders, whose former restaurant Fugaise was a cult hit in a dreadful location, wins and retains fans with food that is impeccably balanced and perfectly edited—if an ingredient's on a plate, it's there for a reason, and it's in harmony with the dish as a whole. The restaurant's name is a nod to the quarterly menu changes, which harness not just Upper Midwestern seasonal ingredients but also intriguing and luxurious tastes from around the world.

Isles Bun & Coffee, 1424 W. 28th St., Minneapolis, MN 55408; (612) 870-4466; islesbun.com; Bakery; $. Traditionally speaking, puppy dog tails are nursery rhyme material, not food to be coveted. And yet Isles Bun & Coffee turns them out to the enthusiastic embrace of the local crowd. They're sweet twists of dough with warm, moist cinnamon centers, humanely portioned and topped with optional dollops of cream cheese frosting made available in a plastic tub near the little cafe's door. Caramel sticky buns, caramel pecan buns, and big-ass cinnamon buns round out the bakery menu, all of which pack much the same delicious punch as the tails, albeit in far heftier packages.

It's Greek to Me, 626 W. Lake St., Minneapolis, MN 55408; (612) 825-9922; itsgreektomemn.com; Greek; $$. There are certain restaurant names that inspire confidence, and It's Greek to Me isn't one of them—it implies a sort of fly-by-night schtickyness. And yet It's Greek to Me is a rock-solid performer, holding down its patch of turf for more than 25 years, serving up everything from *tzatziki* (yogurt cucumber dip), to *saganaki* (flaming cheese) and *souvlaki* (charbroiled, marinated pork loin). The atmosphere is staid but comfortable, particularly for the otherwise loud and clubby norm that dominates Uptown, and the food rates reliably between decent and delicious.

Jasmine Deli, 2532 Nicollet Ave., Minneapolis, MN 55404; (612) 870-4700; Vietnamese, $. Small, soulful, a bit grungy, and a great bargain—this walk-in closet of a restaurant has many affectionate followers who appreciate its tasty broken rice plates, its simple but tasty *banh mi*, and its rock-bottom prices. Most Vietnamese and Chinese restaurants in the Twin Cities offer mock duck as a veg- etarian option, but Jasmine Deli really pushes it, and they know how to handle the sometimes tricky protein. Service is friendly (if not gregarious) and makes for a smooth transition into the first-gener- ation Vietnamese environment of the deli. You eat like a student if you come here, but a very smart student with a refined global palate.

Jax Cafe, 1928 University Ave. Northeast, Minneapolis, MN 55418; (612) 789-7297; jaxcafe.com; Steak House; $$$$. As old-school as they come, Jax steak house is practically encrusted with more than 75 years of comfort, tradition, and easygoing luxury. Make a reservation a few days in advance and everyone in your party will be presented with a custom-printed matchbook featuring the restaurant's name and the name of the person who made the reservation. The eatery's palpable '50s glamour vibe led local DJ Jake Rudh to throw a season three *Mad Men* kickoff party at the restaurant in 2009, and the restaurant's arboreal patio is a go-to spot for graduations and wedding-related festivities. The menu is proudly dated, with beer-can chicken, jumbo shrimp cocktail, grilled Reubens, and other old standbys serving as necessary padding before the onslaught of steak that defines the feel of the place. And if you're looking for a very late lunch or extremely early supper, Jax is your spot—the early-bird dinner menu starts being served at 3:30 p.m. Sun through Fri.

King & I Thai, 1346 LaSalle Ave., Minneapolis, MN 55403; (612) 332-6928; kingandithai.com; Thai; $$. The 30-year-old The King and I Thai doesn't have the salty, hole-in-the-wall charm of some of the Cities' newer, closer-to-the-first-generation Thai restaurants, but it has built a loyal following over the years with its dark, loungey atmosphere and lengthy cocktail list. Party, celebration, and family menus simplify the planning of larger gatherings, and while the King and I Thai's food is pricey and lacks some of the gritty vibrancy of more rustic restaurants, the flavors are nicely balanced and comfortable for those familiar with Thai-American favorites ranging from Pad Thai to fried rice and red curry.

Kings Wine Bar, 4555 Grand Ave. South, Minneapolis, MN 55419; (612) 354-7928; kingsmpls.com; New American; $$. The menu at

Kings Wine Bar leads off with house-made tater tots with gruyere and bacon sauce, and they're a fine symbol of what the place is all about—high class and low brow playfully jumbled together to make a comfortable but elegant living-room-like environment for diners and drinkers. The food is hearty and relatively simple but always a bit elevated or given a clever twist, and the wine list is extensive and reasonably priced, with most bottles clocking in at between $20 and $40. Long on comfort, it's a fine choice for visitors looking to unwind and rub shoulders with the locals.

Leaning Tower of Pizza, 2501 University Ave. Southeast, Minneapolis, MN 55414; (612) 331-7474; leaningtowermpls.com; Pizza; $$. If Punch and Pizza Nea are sleek, modern, and trendy, the Leaning Tower of Pizza is the opposite—rough hewn, unpretentious, and beloved by students and working folks for its high value quotient and fits-like-an-old-pair-of-jeans comfort and ambiance. You won't feel pushed out of a Leaning Tower of Pizza by the rush of crowds or speedy service—your old-school, Midwestern-style medium-crusted pizza arrives when it's good and ready, and you'll like it that way. Ingredients and special pizzas are traditional—the Holy Trinity of Cheese is particularly appropriate for a state that shares a border with Wisconsin, and it boasts mozzarella, cheddar, and parmesan . . . and plenty of all of it. Other Italian-American favorites like spaghetti and meatballs and cheesy bread present like working-class champs—no frills, but solid, filling, and profoundly comforting. **Additional location:** 2324 Lyndale Ave. South, Minneapolis, MN 55405; (612) 377-3532.

Longfellow Grill, 2990 W. River Pkwy., Minneapolis, MN 55406; (612) 721-2711; longfellowgrill.com; American; $$. Casual as can be but boasting an extensive draught beer menu and breakfast-through-late-night dining 7 days a week, the Longfellow is the workhorse next-door eatery for the neighborhood of the same name. Its expansive patio overlooks the Mississippi, and in summertime it fills up with people enjoying its upscale burgers, spins on homey ol' meat loaf, and other accessible, filling treats.

Loring Pasta Bar, 327 14th Ave. Southeast, Minneapolis, MN 55414; (612) 378-4849; loringpastabar.com; Italian; $$. In terms of sheer beauty, it's difficult to top the Loring Pasta Bar. This mid-range Italian restaurant in the University of Minnesota's Dinkytown is a go-to for events ranging from informal reunions all the way up to wedding receptions, largely due to its atmosphere, which evokes a French art nouveau bistro destroyed by bombing and rebuilt into a dark, intriguingly eclectic Italian restaurant. A strong, moderately priced wine selection complements workmanlike but satisfying Italian favorites. An explicitly student-friendly atmosphere and student discounts plus live music and DJs mean that the joint is likely to be jumpin' when you visit, so be prepared for a lively visit in charming surroundings.

Los Ocampo, 809 E. Lake St., Minneapolis, MN 55407; (612) 825-4978; losocampo.com; Mexican; $. One of the best-kept secrets of Minneapolis is its extensive Mexican food scene—to know it, you've got to go to the taquerias of East Lake Street and do a bit of exploring. Your best bet is to start with established, bustling places like taqueria Los Ocampo, which has three locations on Lake Street and two in St. Paul. The huarache (a fried cornmeal cake smothered in refried beans and cheese) is a soulful delight, and the carnitas taco is one of the best in the area. **Additional locations:** 417 E. Lake St., Minneapolis, MN 55407; (612) 823-5398; 920 E. Lake St., Minneapolis, MN 55407; (612) 872-8562; 895 Arcade St., St. Paul, MN 55106; (651) 774-7623; 1751 Suburban Ave., St. Paul, MN 55106; (651) 256-2932.

The Lowbrow, 4244 Nicollet Ave., Minneapolis, MN 55409; (612) 208-0720; thelowbrowmpls.com; American; $$. With an artsy-craftsy decor that suggests Paul Bunyan-meets-The Shins and a comfortable, approachable menu that touts "burgers, beer, and brunch," The Lowbrow is the sort of neighborhood place that you can slouch on into with comfort and hang around in until you've picked bits of bacon out of the remnants of your bacon scallion scramble. There are some clever touches, foodwise (like the Elvis Sandwich, made of bananas, bacon, and peanut butter on grilled sourdough), but by and large the place lives up to its name: easy, uncomplicated, and welcoming to all . . . except, perhaps, snobs.

Lucia's Restaurant, Wine Bar, Bakery, and Take Home, 1432 W. 31st St., Minneapolis, MN 55408; (612) 825-1572; lucias .com; New American; $$$. Bringing the farm to the table for more than 25 years, Lucia's (and its attached bakery) is one of the cornerstones of the local high-end dining establishment, and among the first to recognize that the strength of Upper Midwestern food is using Upper Midwestern agricultural products in a fresh and seasonal way. The ambiance in the restaurant is tasteful and upscale and the food both uncomplicated and elegant, working with limited palates of good ingredients yoked in tandem to achieve a common goal. The next-door bakery space bustles on weekends (and many weekdays) and serves up some of the tastier croissants, popovers, and sweet treats (try the nutty, spiced baby Budapest muffins) in the city.

Lucy's Ethiopian Restaurant, 3025 E. Franklin Ave., Minneapolis, MN 55406; (612) 344-5829; Ethiopian; $. Restaurants don't come any humbler than Lucy's, an Ethiopian joint in the Seward neighborhood frequented by cabbies and known for its big plates of richly spiced African favorites. Ambiance is minimal and service irregular, but prices are low, serving sizes very big indeed, and the authenticity factor through the roof. Crispy, crunchy, vibrant samosas and *tibs*-style sautéed meat dishes are seductive, but Lucy's vegetarian sampler for two is the best buy of the lot, featuring wonderful *shiro* (*berbere*-spiced chickpeas and fried onions) and soulful lentils, all served with spongy *injera* bread.

THE CANDY STORE BOOM

A nostalgia for all things sweet has been sweeping the Twin Cities in recent years, and there have been booms in cupcakes, macarons, doughnuts, and, to boil the sugar craving down to its essence, good old-fashioned candy. South Minneapolis has seen a resurgence of newly founded shops, and the candy addict in downtown Minneapolis or St. Paul has some long-standing options to pick from as well.

Candyland (two locations in downtown Minneapolis at 811 LaSalle Court and on the Dayton Radisson Arcade on 7th Street between Nicollet and Hennepin and one in downtown St. Paul at 435 Wabasha St. North) is the go-to git-'er-done candy shop for shoppers on a mission. It's packed floor to ceiling with nuts, popcorn (in giant bags and tins), chocolates, and a variety of candy products that veer toward the classic and utilitarian (as opposed to the fancy or hard-to-find).

Sugar Sugar (3803 Grand Ave. South, Minneapolis) is part of the new wave of sweets shops, and it goes in for nostalgia in a big way, offering a curated selection of treats guaranteed to appeal to just about any kid and a wide range of cultured and/or nostalgic adults. Founder Joni Wheeler has tricked the shop out in a mix of French vintage, American nostalgia, and Japanese pop, and stocked it with candies that emphasize (alternatively) high-end modern taste and old-fashioned sugary delights barely remembered (Sifers Valomilk, anyone?).

The newly opened **Candy Alley** (4813 Chicago Ave. South, Minneapolis) is worth a stop if you're vintage candy diving and already happen to be in the neighborhood of Sugar Sugar (or vice versa). This cute little boutique offers more than 50 flavors of saltwater taffy and old favorites like Boston Baked Beans, Now and Laters, Slo Pokes, and nostalgia soda including Moxie and Bubble UP.

The Alice In Wonderland-inspired decor of **Alix in Candyland** (5400 France Ave. South, Edina) helps set the scene for a magical adventure in sweets, but the experience doesn't come cheap—along with its desirable Edina location comes a somewhat stiff price tag for the goods. Cute gift boxes, jewelry, and other sidelines help diversify the offerings and make the store an enjoyable place to browse around, whatever your age.

Dulceria La Pinata (1515 E. Lake St.—Lake Street and Bloomington Avenue in Minneapolis), as its name suggests, is your go-to destination for obtaining and stuffing an authentic Mexican pinata. Dozens of the things hang from the ceiling of the store, creating a joyous atmosphere, and there is bin after bin of Mexican bulk candy available for purchasing and stuffing your new, breakable animal friend. As an added bonus, Dulceria La Pinata is located inside of the south-of-the-border themed Mercado Central, meaning that you're a few purposeful footsteps away from *tacos al pastor* at Taqueria la Hacienda.

Manny's Tortas, 920 E. Lake St., Minneapolis, MN 55407; (612) 870-3930; mannystortas.com; Mexican; $. The richly flavored, profoundly hearty, gloriously grilled sandwich known as the *torta* is a bit of a Minneapolis thing, thanks in part to the high number of Mexican immigrants in South Minneapolis, and to the influence of Manny's Tortas. The genius of Manny's is taking a favorite Mexico City street food, the *torta*, and turning it into a clearly described ("Gourmet Mexican Sandwiches"), reliably prepared commodity that appeals equally to native Mexicans and the population of Minneapolis at large. The sandwiches come loaded with cheese, tomato, lettuce, onion, avocado, jalapeños, refried beans, chipotle pepper mayo, and various proteins including eggs with Mexican sausage, breaded steak (the Milanesa), pork loin, chicken, and the Hawaiian (ham and pineapple). If you're in or near the Midtown Global Market, this is a hell of a way to do lunch.

Market Bar-B-Que, 1414 Nicollet Ave. South, Minneapolis, MN 55403; (612) 872-1111; marketbbq.com; Barbecue; $$. The twin cities of Minneapolis and St. Paul aren't known for their barbecue culture, and Market Bar-B-Que won't radically change visitors' minds on that front (for a place that might, see **Q Fanatic**, p. 114). That said: The restaurant makes respectable 'cue that deserves patronage, its pit-smoked ribs are sufficiently tasty that they merit sampling, and the restaurant's rib tips are made with sufficient confidence that they're served with sauce on the side (generally a good sign of a barbecue joint's overall skill level). The pulled pork is similarly good, notable for its moist and tender texture.

Marla's Caribbean Cuisine, 3761 Bloomington Ave., Minneapolis, MN 55407; (612) 724-3088; marlascuisine.com; Caribbean; $. Everything about Marla's Caribbean Cuisine is humble except for the flavor, which is skyrockets at night in terms of its depth and oomph. The restaurant is true to its roots in Trinidad and Tobago, serving up humble but zesty dishes with sides of beans and rice in an environment often permeated by authentic radio chatter and music piped in from the islands via the Internet. Doubles (soft fried bread surrounding Indian-style curried chickpeas) make for the perfect start to a meal, which will likely be some sort of stewed chicken, fish, or even goat.

Masa, 1070 Nicollet Mall, Minneapolis, MN 55403; (612) 338-6272; masa-restaurant.com; Mexican; $$$. Proximate to the headquarters of the Target Corporation and any number of other prominent downtown office parks, Masa is the perfect power lunch spot: upscale enough to impress, casual enough to avoid stressing anyone out, ethnic enough to intrigue with its Mexican-American-nouveau style, but safe enough to offer recognizable favorites that even a Republican visiting from Bismarck can identify and enjoy. Margaritas, sangria, tequilas, and *aguas frescas* make for a formidable and coherent libations menu, and the wine list is long and ambitious. All dishes are thoughtful and involve at least one or two pleasing twists, and while the overall experience is expensive enough to make an expense account a nice way to pad the blow, it's not exorbitant for the quality of food received.

The menu offers a good balance between tricked-out street food (enchiladas, tamales, tacos) and *platillo fuertes*, entrees with real substance.

Masu Sushi & Robata, 330 E. Hennepin Ave., Minneapolis, MN 55414; (612) 332-6278; masusushiandrobata.com; Japanese; $$$. Any place where you can bring visiting San Francisco–based food journalists and get an enthusiastic thumbs-up on the sushi is OK by me. This recently opened Japanese eatery prides itself on doing sustainable sushi, but the lack of endangered fish hasn't handicapped it at all in the flavor department—rolls and nigiri here are melt-in-your-mouth tender, with perfectly seasoned and textured rice, and well-balanced proportions of ingredients. The menu goes far beyond raw fish, however—Masu serves up a pork katsu ramen that is among the tastiest in town, and a wide variety of small bar-style noshes and *robata* (skewered meats and/or vegetables) that make great shared small plates. Set meals can make a visit to Masu a feast of many flavors, or you can easily pick and choose all night from the menu, which is ambitious but well organized. Nipponophiles will go nuts three times when they come here: once when they taste the food, again when they take in the high-style sleek kitsch of the pachinko machine and sci-fi kewpie doll decor, and a third

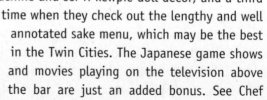

time when they check out the lengthy and well annotated sake menu, which may be the best in the Twin Cities. The Japanese game shows and movies playing on the television above the bar are just an added bonus. See Chef

Chase's recipe for **Ginger Duck Gyoza with Ponzu Plum Sauce (Japanese Pot Stickers)** on page 243.

Mazopiya Natural Food Market, 2571 Credit Union Dr., Prior Lake, MN 55372; (952) 233-9140; mazopiya.com; Organic Food Store; $$. Established by the Shakopee Mdewakanton Sioux Community Tribal Council across the street from Mystic Lake Casino, the geothermally heated and silver LEED certified Mazopiya Natural Food Market is neck and neck with cutting-edge co-ops like Seward and Linden Hills in terms of providing healthy whole foods in well-lighted, comfortable environments. Modern as it is, the market represents a back-to-tradition approach to eating for members of the tribe—while modern Native American diets suffer from many of the high-fat, high-salt, high-cholesterol problems as all American diets, original Native American eating patterns tended to favor much simpler and less processed food, like the kind available at Mazopiya. It also represents "food sovereignty" by providing healthy food in an area where obtaining any groceries whatsoever used to require a 4-mile drive.

Merlin's Rest, 3601 E. Lake St., Minneapolis, MN 55406; (612) 216-2419; merlinsrest.com; British Isles; $$. It's not entirely clear how an authentic Scottish/Irish pub ended up on East Lake Street, but that's Merlin's Rest for you: 50 percent real, and 50 percent inexplicable. Founded by British Isles ex-pats, Merlin's

Rest is steeped in dark wood, whimsical signage, and the type of affable blather that makes visiting a real pub a respite for the soul. Although the British Isles–inflected menu is nothing to write home about, Merlin's Rest has one of the finest single malt whiskey lists in the area and a fine collection of beers on draught. As an added bonus, Merlin's Rest boasts what is most certainly the most grueling pub trivia night in the Cities, overseen by author and "minister of culture" Bill Watkins. A score in the high twenties (out of 100 percent) is admirable, and a score in the high thirties may put you in position to win—and this is amid the very smart crowd of government, IT people, and intellectual masochists who tend to turn out for this level of abuse.

Mill Valley Kitchen, 3906 Excelsior Blvd., St. Louis Park, MN 55416; (952) 358-2000; millvalleykitchen.com; New American; $$$. California diet spa fare meets the well-heeled Minneapolis suburbs at the Mill Valley Kitchen, a cleanly cut gemstone of a restaurant with superfluous valet parking and a menu that lists calories and other nutrition information next to each dish served. If you're in the mood to eat light and healthy, Mill Valley does a fine job of presenting options to attain that goal, starting with a mixed green salad with (a very tiny amount of) goat cheese and craisins (250 calories) and wrapping up with dessert miniatures (tiny bites of apple crisp or maple panna cotta). One particularly pleasing touch: Mill Valley offers a variety of juice, tea, and agave nectar and coconut water nonalcoholic cocktails (called "refreshments") that are, indeed, quite refreshing and beautifully balanced.

Modern Cafe, 337 13th Ave. Northeast, Minneapolis, MN 55413; (612) 378-9882; moderncafeminneapolis.com; New American; $$. The Modern Cafe is one of those unassuming little places that draws you in without warning, shows you a damned fine time, and leaves you trying to figure it out after the fact. The decor's polished metal and patterned floor suggest a humble but well-maintained 1940s diner, and while the food is interesting and often straight-up fantastic, there's not a lot of bragging going on, either on the mercifully brief and easy-to-read menu or the website. The soulful, high-end pub-grub-meets-meat-loaf-and-pot-roast-style food does the talking, and that makes for an environment refreshingly free of pretense, where—hurrah!—actual relaxation can take place. And for those who care about local and/or sustainable options, the Modern Cafe is a fine choice, name-checking purveyors on its menu and regularly interfacing with the local food community. (If you ever knew the wonderful B-Side diner in Cambridge, MA, the Modern Cafe might be its long-lost twin.)

Moto-i, 2940 Lyndale Ave. South, Minneapolis, MN 55408; (612) 821-6262; moto-i.com; Japanese Izakaya; $$. Moto-i is the first (and perhaps still only) sake brewpub and restaurant outside of Japan—this means the sake's brewed and served on-site, and the food is focused on Japanese Izakaya fare, not the middlebrow, forgettable sushi that blankets Uptown like a plague. Service and food can be inconsistent (the restaurant is a sizeable, multifloor affair with an active roof deck in the summer), but the drinks menu is consistently pleasing, particularly for sake fans, who will savor the chance to try decent stuff made on-site. The bar snacks are mostly addictive—they include terrific shishito pepper, cream cheese, and bacon rangoons, deeply flavorful Thai beef jerky (made in house), and hoisin pork buns the equal of any in the area. Moto-i is right on trend with its udon and ramen selections, featuring add-ons like fried eggs, fish cakes, chicken, cabbage, and more. The restaurant's loud and dark atmosphere can get overwhelming on the weekends if you're not into that sort of thing, but on the plus side, a vegetarian and allergy-friendly menu makes Moto-i extra friendly for diners with special restrictions.

Mozza Mia Pizza Pie and Mozzarella Bar, 3910 W. 50th St., Minneapolis, MN 55424; (952) 288-2882; mozzamia.com; Italian; $$. Offering house-made mozzarella, pasta, and light wood-fired pizzas, Mozza Mia is an upscale alternative to chain or traditional Midwestern pizza joints. The mozzarella won't reshape your world, but if you've got a big group or clamorous kids, the boisterous atmosphere and simple food is sure to please. As is true for all restaurants in the Parasole chain, when you dine at Mozza Mia expect slick presentation, well-thought-through menus, and a reasonably hefty check at the end of the meal.

Muddy Waters, 2401 Lyndale Ave. South, Minneapolis, MN 55405; (612) 872-2232; muddywaters.food.officelive.com; Gastropub; $$. A mere coffeehouse once upon a time, Muddy Waters has moved forward into a brave new world of gastronomy and now operates as a full-service bar and restaurant in the heart of Uptown. Best described as a gastropub, Muddy Waters boasts a serious selection of local and national draught beers, and a broad, eclectic range of snacks and entrees that allow a diner to nosh for hours or have a proper meal amid the restaurant's stylish and noisy interior.

My Burger, 601 Marquette Ave. #206, Minneapolis, MN 55402; (612) 436-033; myburgerusa.com; Burgers; $. Well in advance of the current "better burger" explosion (think the rapid expansions of Five Guys, In-N-Out, and Smashburger) came  Minneapolis's own My Burger, a local fast-food joint known for its semi-fancy, quickly made lunchtime sandwiches. Occasional special Burgers of the Month spice up its spartan menu. Atmosphere is nuts-and-bolts, too—a clean, well-maintained space, but not a place to sit down and savor a meal. The downtown location is a favorite spot of Skyway dwellers, the Minneapolitans who stick to heated, covered, elevated passageways that connect downtown buildings and make venturing out into the arctic cold unnecessary. **Additional location:** 3100 Excelsior, Minneapolis, MN 55416; (612) 746-0800.

Northeast Social, 359 13th Ave. Northeast, Minneapolis, MN 55413; (612) 877-8111; northeastsocial.com; New American; $$. Like its next door neighbor the **Modern Cafe** (p. 99), Northeast

Social brings sophisticated flavors to hearty, soulful entrees, although Northeast Social leans a little more firmly on haute cuisine techniques and ingredients with the likes of duck liver mousse, beef carpaccio, and pumpkin gnocchi. And when the bell at the bar rings, raise your glass and toast "to the Social!"—it's part of the restaurant's tradition. (As of publication, Northeast Social was at work opening a sister restaurant on Nicollet Avenue called Eat Street Social.)

Obento-Ya Japanese Bistro, 1510 Como Ave. Southeast, Minneapolis, MN 55414; (612) 331-1432; obento-ya.com; Japanese; $$. This charming little restaurant near the University of Minnesota's Minneapolis campus is a favorite spot for lunching faculty and visiting alumni, combining a quiet, gracious atmosphere with a very with-it interpretation of Japanese pub grub and *robata* (skewered meat and/or vegetables). The menu has entrees and set meals, but its real appeal is how easy it is to customize a meal from the many offerings on hand, from small, savory *robata* skewers to sushi rolls to dumplings to noodle dishes. In the summer, a backyard garden patio is a fine way to enjoy the sunshine, and in the winter there's nothing more comforting than a hot cup of tea and a big steaming bowl of udon. The regular specials are always worth exploring and often put a fresh, seasonal spin on regular menu items that is most welcome.

Oceanaire Seafood Room, 1300 Nicollet Ave., Minneapolis, MN 55403; (612) 333-2277; theoceanaire.com; Seafood; $$$$. Once the preeminent seafood restaurant in the Twin Cities, Oceanaire has had to grapple with a major change in ownership and stiff competition from the likes of the newly opened **Sea Change** (p. 124) and **Meritage**'s new oyster bar (p. 151). Still, for a high-end classic seafood meal, few restaurants can match Oceanaire's luxe menu and professional service. An ambitious wine list and spare-no-expense entrees make this a place for anniversary splurges and high-powered tete-a-tetes. Like other top-of-the-line seafood eateries here, the fish is flown in daily, so while it's not quite the same as oceanside seafood dining, it's the next best thing: air hub seafood dining. With seafood, freshness is key, but proper presentation is right up there—Oceanaire's plating and display are flamboyant and elegant.

112 Eatery, 112 N. 3rd St., Minneapolis, MN 55401; (612) 343-7696; 112eatery.com; American; $$. Only somewhat supplanted (or perhaps just supplemented?) by its swanky Warehouse District sibling **Bar La Grassa** (p. 51), 112 Eatery is an anomaly on the Twin Cities dining scene: It's open late (full kitchen service as late as 1 a.m. on weekends). It's chic without being pretentious, boasting a young, energetic atmosphere that gets boisterous even into the latter part of the evening. And it sells generously portioned high-end food at mid-range prices. Throw in some addictive menu mainstays such as fresh pasta with rich, silken chicken and *foie* *gras* meatballs or beautifully executed and absurdly decadent *tres leches* cake, and you've got a barn-burner of a restaurant that has been doing steady to enthusiastic business since it opened in 2009. 112 Eatery Chef Isaac Becker was named Best Chef in the Midwest by the James Beard Awards in 2011, and he is deeply immersed in the Twin Cities food scene; while there isn't much of a sense of Midwestern place to the menu, it feels vibrant, cosmopolitan, and contemporary, albeit in a small space that isn't terrific for large groups. In short: If you're a traveler staying downtown with limited time and money, 112 is one of the best ways to spend your evening and dining budget.

Origami & Origami West, 30 N. 1st St. #1, Minneapolis, MN 55401; (612) 333-8430; origamirestaurant.com; Japanese; $$$. High-end, fresh-tasting sushi is the hallmark of this Japanese restaurant duo, known by many locals as some of the best in the state. It's one of the few restaurants in the Twin Cities where ordering *omakase* (chef's choice) is both possible and recommended—it may in fact be the best way to take advantage of the restaurant's freshest fish and enjoy some surprises along the way. Decor and atmosphere are pleasant and minimalist, and while it's not the best place to get a sake buzz going, that's a double-edged sword—those in search of a civilized meal will find Origami's sense of calm pleasing when compared to some its more rowdy contemporaries. **Additional location:** 12305 Wayzata Blvd., Minnetonka, MN 55305; (952) 746-3398.

The Original Pancake House, 3501 W. 70th St., Edina, MN 55435; (952) 920-4444; originalpancakehouse.com; Breakfast; $$. The reason this national chain merits mention is that its overall quality of food far exceeds what you might expect from a mini-breakfast empire that stretches from Niagara Falls to Hawaii. Real butter and serious culinary love go into the extensive menu, which features some delightful specialty items such as cheesy *roesti* potatoes and the "Dutch baby," an eggy, almost custard-like oven-baked pancake typical of Holland. I can only personally vouch for the Edina location, but if the other two local spots are similar in tone, expect pleasingly mild but flavorful coffee, attentive service, and a warm, homey decor and atmosphere. If you're coming for breakfast on a weekend, either show up before 9 a.m. or be prepared to put some time in—OPH can get seriously crowded. **Additional locations:** 549 Prairie Center Dr., Eden Prairie, MN 55344; (952) 224-9440; 6322 Vinewood Lane, Osseo, MN 55311; (763) 383-0888.

Our Kitchen, 813 W. 36th St., Minneapolis, MN 55408; (612) 825-3718; Diner; $. There aren't many places like Our Kitchen left: truly old-school, tiny, lived-in breakfast dives that recall a bygone era. This worn-down greasy spoon serves big portions of classic American breakfasts, including biscuits and gravy (some of the most convincing in the Cities), crispy hash browns, endless coffee, thick-cut french toast, bacon, eggs, and toast. Food can take awhile to emerge from the restaurant's small kitchen, and there's nothing special about Our Kitchen's limited breakfast-focused menu, but those in love with simplicity and value will find its humble approach to gastronomy refreshing and satisfying. It's also a refreshing change of pace from most of the rest of Uptown, which tends to be trend-driven to the point of inducing madness.

Pairings Food and Wine Market, 6001 Shady Oak Rd. South, Minnetonka, MN 55343; (952) 426-0522; pairingsfoodandwine.com; Deli; $$. Part deli and part liquor and wine store, Pairings does a fine job of bringing together food and spirits. On the food side, Pairings keeps it clean and simple—a cobb salad, wraps, sandwiches, light pastas, and classic pizzas. On the spirits side, a fine collection of local beers joins the room of well-curated wines, and an ongoing series of happy hours and educational sessions helps to introduce the public to the fruit of the vine (or of the malted grain).

Pannekoeken Dutch Family, 1845 County Rd. D E, Maplewood, MN 55109; (651) 779-7844; Breakfast; $$. If you're in the neighborhood of a Pannekoeken Dutch Family restaurant and game for a different kind of breakfast, stop on by—this somewhat dingy chain serves up a pleasing variety of eggy, oven-baked Dutch-style pancakes called *pannekoeken*. While the atmosphere is nothing to write home about, the food is comforting, amusing, filling, and novel. **Additional location:** 4995 Excelsior Blvd., Minneapolis, MN 55416; (952) 920-2120.

Patisserie 46, 4552 Grand Ave. South, Minneapolis, MN 55419; (612) 354-3257; patisserie46.com; Bakery; $$. Though recently opened, this European-style bakery in the Kingfield neighborhood has captured the hearts of the Cities' gourmets, who nearly unanimously admire its impeccable attention to detail, balanced flavor profiles, and tendency to put natural fruit and delicately turned out pastry first, rather than simply killing its baked goods with sickening sweet glazes and frostings. Flakey croissants, caneles, macarons, almond financiers, and more stock the bakery's jaw-droppingly elegant case, and coffee and some light, sandwich-focused meals are available for those who want to linger. A generally Continental vibe makes the lingering pleasant. If you're a sophisticated sweets fiend, Patisserie 46 is well worth a drive if you have opportunity.

Patrick's Bakery and Cafe, 2928 W. 66th St., Richfield, MN; (612) 861-7570; patricksbakerycafe.com; Bakery; $$. The baked goods at Patrick's are directly informed by the sensibilities of Europe—the bakery's founder, Patrick Bernet, is a classically trained baker who served as a pastry instructor at the Cordon Bleu in Paris. Those sensibilities translate to delicately worked dough, light, natural flavors, and a pleasant absence of the sort of gooey sugary mess that brings down so many American baked goods. Patrick's Bakery, located in the heart of the sprawling Lyndale Avenue location of Bachman's Floral, makes for a uniquely restorative in-town winter getaway—to sip coffee and munch on subtle, finely crafted pastries on wrought-iron tables while surrounded by green growing things, yellow parasols, and vibrant flowers is a powerful tonic amid sub-zero temperatures and drifting walls of snow. **Additional location:** 6010 S. Lyndale Ave. (in Bachman's), Minneapolis, MN; (612) 861-9277.

The Return of the Craft Cocktail

Once upon a time, before Prohibition, making a cocktail was an art form. Drinks weren't sugary abominations, relying upon heavy mixers and sweet flavor to kill the taste of bad (often illicitly made and sold) liquor—they put good alcohol first, accented and dressed up with bitters and other sophisticated mixers that accentuated and played with the natural strengths of the beverage at hand.

"Pre-Prohibition" has become a password in the cocktail industry for doing drinks with a sense of balance, restraint, and top-shelf booze, and a number of Twin Cities restaurants and bars have embraced the movement.

Mixologist Johnny Michaels (author of the book *North Star Cocktails*) is the area's leading bartending consultant, having put together cocktail menus for a number of the Twin Cities' most prominent restaurants including **La Belle Vie** (p. 29), **Masu Sushi & Robata** (p. 96), **Cafe Maude** (p. 62), **Barrio** (p. 52), **Smalley's** (p. 173), and others. His imprint is unmistakable—drinks with unusual names (often inspired by Smiths songs) and sophisticated syrups and bitters that play up high-quality spirits.

Heartland's bartending program is one of the strongest in the Cities—its staff slings classics as well as anyone else, but also do groundbreaking work like creating local black walnut–infused liquor for use in unique cocktails. The bar at **Heartland** (p. 148) is one of the busiest in St. Paul, and a favorite place for an upscale after-work drink.

The **Marvel Bar** (beneath the newly opened and remarkable **Bachelor Farmer** restaurant, p. 48) is a dark den of hipness, downright difficult to find and enter from the street and staffed by mustachioed and be-hatted bartenders who self-consciously evoke a bygone era. Its drinks are often challenging, tend toward the strong, and are guaranteed to be entertaining to anyone who is up for a new experience—any bar that can make a blend of olive oil, egg white, lemon, Licor 43, and gin (the Oliveto) into a successful and balanced drink deserves kudos.

The retro lounge known as the **Bradstreet Craftshouse** (p. 56) wears its dedication to good drinks on its sleeve—from its heavy use of rye whiskey (typical of pre-Prohibition cocktails) to its addition of ingredients via the exacting use of eyedropper, the ritzy hotel bar brings the art of beverages to a high plane. That a New York–based drinks consultancy got the Crafthouse off the ground is no shame—the local staff keeps the quality up for a demanding clientele, many of whom are staying in the attached Graves hotel for business travel.

Pho Tau Bay, 2837 Nicollet Ave., Minneapolis, MN 55408; (612) 874-6030; photaubay.us; Vietnamese; $$. When Anthony Bourdain comes to Minneapolis and St. Paul, the cuisine he seeks out is Vietnamese, and that's not accidental—southeast Asian immigrants have brought the vibrant, funky, spicy, balanced food of their homelands to the area with a passion. Pho Tau Bay is one of the places that's best bridging the gap between the home country and the locals, and you'll see a half-Asian, half-Anglo customer base on a typical visit. In cold weather, the offerings of Pho Tau Bay really shine—big bowls of pho with sprouts, cilantro, sauces, and other options for a customizable meal, of course, but also broken rice plates with superb grilled pork, and Chinese-style entrees like lo mein and spicy duck dishes. The atmosphere is casual at best, but the dining room is spacious and can handle a big crowd.

Pizza Luce, 119 N. 4th St., Minneapolis, MN 55401; (612) 333-7359; plus numerous other locations in the Cities; pizzaluce .com; Pizza; $$. It's hard to escape Pizza Luce, the tattooed hipster–staffed semi-fancy pizza chain that projects its influence throughout the urban area. Slickly marketed and bedecked with interesting ingredients (garlic mashed potatoes, veggie ball crumbles, pico de gallo, shrimp and pesto, etc.) and flavor combinations, this stuff stands out from frozen or chain pizzas, in a good way, and has built a loyal following.

Pizza Nea, 306 E. Hennepin Ave., Minneapolis, MN 55414; (612) 331-9298; pizzanea.com; Pizza; $$. That Neapolitan-style Pizza Nea is outgunned 7-to-1 by its rival **Punch** (p. 113) can't be explained by the food—both restaurants use top-notch ingredients and ultra-hot ovens to make delicate, thin-crust pizzas that pop with cheesy flavor. Nea, it should be said, may be even more aggressive about piling on daunting but effective combinations of ingredients, and at avoiding the soggy center phenomenon that is either Punch's downfall or charming quirk, depending on who you ask. Nea's atmosphere is clean and modern with interior brick walls and light hardwood floors, the service professional and generally charming, and the specials board always worth consulting for the latest ambitious attempt to make pizza history. All pizzas *rossa* (red pizzas) are made with crushed San Marzano tomatoes and fresh mozzarella, and any of the restaurant's pizzas can be made into a calzone upon request.

Pizzeria Lola, 5557 Xerxes Ave. S, Minneapolis, MN 55410; (612) 424-8338; pizzerialola.com; Pizza; $$. Helmed by International School of Pizza–trained Ann Kim, Pizzeria Lola burst onto the scene in late 2010, opening to a packed dining room that still hasn't yet really calmed down very much. Kim's certification matters; her school is the only US affiliate of Italy's respected Scuola Italiana Pizzaioli, and the results of her education can be seen and tasted in the pizzeria's product, which is thin, crispy, chewy, beautifully flame-kissed, and well balanced in terms of toppings, crust, and sauce. The shop's modern decor is anchored by a jaw-droppingly gorgeous copper wood-fired oven, and while the crowds are fierce,

tables turn relatively quickly—the pizzas come fast and furious. Lola dishes up easily one of the best 10 pizzas in the Twin Cities—arguably in the top 5, and while it's a neighborhood-anchored place by location, it draws clientele from all around the Cities.

Porter & Frye, 1115 2nd Ave. S, Minneapolis, MN 55403; (612) 353-3500; porterandfrye.com; American; $$$. A viable contender for "most underrated restaurant in the Twin Cities," Porter & Frye has the bad luck to be linked to a hotel, albeit the swanky Hotel Ivy. Hotel restaurants are perceived as sterile, overpriced, and enslaved to trends, hostage to their own captive audiences of bored business travelers from Omaha and Des Moines. Porter & Frye Chef Sarah Master, by contrast, has managed to create a menu that incorporates local and seasonal produce and lively flourishes. The cocktail menu is another surprising strength—try *El Pelon* (the bald man), a beautifully balanced roller coaster of flavor consisting of Don Julio silver tequila, fresh cucumber, lime, and jalapeño. And the chef's table is a gastronomic pleasure, prepared in a thoughtfully and refreshingly non-stuffy way. The feel of the place is defined by clean, modern, business-friendly ambiance and pleasantly professional servers. See Chef Master's recipes for **Chèvre Cheesecake** on p. 252 and **Bison Reuben** on p. 254.

Psycho Suzi's, 1900 Marshall St. NE, Minneapolis, MN 55418; (612) 788-9069; Tiki Bar; $$$. Don't come to the rip-roaringly popular Psycho Suzi's tiki bar and restaurant for the passable bar food or even the drinks, which are syrup-sweet and underpowered. Come for the carnival-like Polynesian-themed atmosphere, the ridiculous mugs and glasses that hold the drinks, and—in warm weather—the sprawling riverside patio that ranks among the finest in the city. Throngs feel right at home here, so if you've got a big group, brave the crowds and join the party. If you've got to order something to eat, try the pizzas, which are pleasantly greasy thin-crusted bar-style wonders that line the stomach for the onslaught of a drink or three.

Pumphouse Creamery, 4754 Chicago Ave. S, Minneapolis, MN 55407; (612) 825-2021; pumphouse-creamery.com; Ice Cream; $. The handmade, organic, all-natural ice cream sold by Pumphouse Creamery is made on-site, and this cute little ice cream shop has plenty of local fans. Flavors incorporate novel ingredients (buckwheat honey, pumpkin, local craft beer) to serve up new experiences that embrace the community and the region. Nonhomogenized organic cream top dairy from Crystal Ball Farm in Osceola, Wisconsin, is at the heart of all of Pumphouse's scoops.

Punch Neapolitan Pizza, 3226 W Lake St., (612) 929-0006 plus numerous other locations in the Cities; punchpizza.com; Pizza; $$. Open since 1996, Punch is the big gorilla on the block when it comes to local wood-fired pizza, and it's VPN-certified to boot—that means the flour, the cheese, and the tomato sauce meet Italian ingredient standards, and the oven reaches an infernal 800°F as it turns San Marzano tomatoes and fresh mozz into tasty pizza in what seems like seconds. Italian decorating touches make Punch a pleasant place to inhale pizza at—the quick service and fleeting nature of a hot VPN pizza means you probably won't linger for too long, regardless of the European deco-framed wall art or the lovely tiled ovens that are the visual centerpieces of any given location. Punch is a master of social media, and if you follow them on Twitter and Facebook (as many thousands do), you'll soon be privy to a number of excellent (and sometimes extremely fast-moving) offers up to and including BOGO or even free pizzas during extreme inclement weather and for other special occasions.

Q Fanatic, 180 Miller Rd., Champlin, MN 55316; (763) 323-6550; qfanatic.com; Barbecue, $$. Minneapolis-St. Paul isn't known for its barbecue, but that's OK—the scene has a lot of other strong points, and you've gotta give the mid-South something to hold on to. That said, there's a little place called Q Fanatic in a strip mall in Champlin—almost entirely devoid of atmosphere or character—overseen by a man named Charlie Johnson. Johnson, a restaurateur, made the not particularly romantic decision to get into barbecue because he saw it as recession-proof, and Q Fanatic was born—a place with some of the most gorgeously smoked ribs and well-balanced sauces (served on the side as a default, mind you) in the region. Competitive (in my experience) quality to real barbecue joints in cities like Chapel Hill and St. Louis, Q Fanatic is a strange outlier, a Twin Cities barbecue joint founded for mercantile reasons that has food with soul. Ribs are king, and try anything with the espresso barbecue sauce or the spicy pepper vodka sauce.

Qoraxlow, 1821 E. Lake St., Minneapolis, MN 55407; no website or phone number; East African; $. This East African restaurant is sufficiently authentic that there's a room for men, a room for women, and a "VIP" room reserved for the odd non-African guest to stop by. (Said guests should also be aware that the VIP room doubles as a prayer room, which can make for a slightly awkward cultural experience.) The food tends toward Mediterranean or Persian, with spiced and raisin-laden rice and generous bounties of beef, chicken, fish, goat, and gyro-like mystery meat available for the curious at heart. Qoraxlow typifies what makes East Lake Street so much fun for the enterprising chow scout—it's a portal to another place.

Rainbow Chinese Restaurant, 2739 Nicollet Ave. South, Minneapolis, MN 55408; (612) 870-7084; rainbowrestaurant.com; Chinese; $$. Generally speaking, Chinese restaurants in the Upper Midwest aren't famed for their use of seasonal, local produce—they're economy joints where people on a budget suck down greasy, affordable, salty food. By contrast, Rainbow Chinese founder Tammy Wong has made a name for herself by not merely using market produce but by energetically putting on cooking demos and market tours that highlight the interrelationship between quality produce and meat and beautifully done Chinese classics. The lush, comfortable setting lends itself well to multicourse noshing on the restaurant's brightly flavored dishes, and the story of the menu is a refreshing change from the depressing standard set by neighborhood Chinese restaurants.

Red Stag Supperclub, 509 1st Ave. Northeast, Minneapolis, MN 55413; (612) 767-7766; redstagsupperclub.com; New American; $$$. A Wisconsin-style supper club is a particular sort of place where the food is straight, unapologetic meat and potatoes, there's always a fish fry on Friday, the Old-Fashioneds are made with brandy (and consumed with alarming frequency), and the decor is so determinedly fusty and uncool as to be ironically hip. Not infrequently, you'll also find chocolate pudding as one of the salad bar choices, for reasons that are obscure to this writer, despite his Wisconsin roots. The Red Stag, which bills itself as an heir to the supper club tradition, is one or two steps removed from that platonic ideal—the food's fancier, made with more haute cuisine care and fuss, and the dining room is modern and sleek, with an open kitchen (absolutely unheard of in the world of traditional supper clubs, which almost universally feel like creatures of the late '50s or early '60s). Breaks from tradition aside, there's a lot worth exploring at the LEED-certified and aggressively locavore Red Stag. For starters, the Friday fish fry offers the often-seen but rarely served bluegill as an option, smelt fries with sweet onion tartar sauce, and the absolutely non-canonical seared scallops with sweet corn and huitlacoche. Dinner ranges from updated classics like bison stroganoff to chi chi comfort food like lobster mac and cheese and truffled kettle corn. And, yes, the brandy Old-Fashioned heads up the cocktails menu.

Rice Paper, 3948 W. 50th St., Edina, MN 55424; (952) 288-2888; ricepaperrestaurant.com; Asian; $$$. Rarified atmosphere and light, delicate, beautifully made little bites typify Rice Paper, a pan-Asian restaurant with a decidedly haute cuisine twist. While it can be a bit shocking in terms of price per pound of food, it makes up for high prices with delicate flavors—its food draws upon touches like tamarind, toasted coconut, jasmine, lemongrass, and more to impart subtle flavor.

Risotto, 610 W. Lake St., Minneapolis, MN 55408; (612) 823-4338; risottomn.com; Italian; $$. Four varieties of this restaurant's eponymous dish grace its menu, along with carefully cropped selections of pasta, and meat-and-potato entrees like a grilled beef tenderloin with rosemary roasted potatoes and a grilled bone-in pork chop with mashed potatoes and a rosemary apple carrot marsala sauce. Dim lighting and cozy surroundings make this a great place for a date or a long, carb-fueled session of manging and catching up, although the noise level can climb on a busy night. The food has won plaudits from diners and critics, none so consistently as the consistently tasty selection of risottos, any of which is a fine winter night's companion.

Riverview Cafe and Wine Bar, 3745 42nd Ave. South, Minneapolis, MN 55406; (612) 722-7234; theriverview.net; Cafe; $$. A neighborhood mainstay just minutes (on foot) from the Mississippi River, the Riverview is a gathering place for students and readers during the day, and bon vivants in search of wine during the evening. The cafe is both cozy-casual and spacious, with nooks for studying and browsing the news, while the wine bar section of the Riverview is a bit spiffier, with dim lighting and a more Manhattan feel to it. The menu features more than 100 different wines from around the world, and the food menu includes pizza and light appetizers.

Ronin Cafe and Sushi Bar, 7704 160th St. West, Lakeville, MN 55044; (952) 997-6646; ronincafe.com; Japanese; $$. An independently owned sushi and noodle eatery located in the southern suburbs, Ronin Cafe distinguishes itself with spirited noodle dishes and by offering true *omakase* (chef's choice), which is purchased by naming a dollar amount and then letting the chefs do the work of picking out your various small tastes of food until your limit has been hit. The atmosphere is unremarkable, but the care put into the food sets Ronin apart from many of its more pro forma "cash in on the sushi train" style competitors in the 'burbs.

Rudolph's Bar-B-Que, 1933 Lyndale Ave. South, Minneapolis, MN 55403; (612) 871-8969; rudolphsribs.com; Barbecue; $$$. For a city with a lot of white people and a lot of black people, Minneapolis doesn't have a lot of restaurants with a racially mixed clientele— geography tends to dictate who you see dining out in any given spot. A happy exception is Rudolph's, a swinging, late-night kind of barbecue restaurant that features big portions, comfortable chairs, a polished menu with a little something for everyone, and sleek decor. While this isn't your disheveled, burned-out, run-down shack of a barbecue joint (read: it's not the world's most soulful and mind-blowing take on the genre), the food is reliably tasty, and many of the sides would serve a high school football team. The rotating vertical sign on the restaurant's interior is almost worth the visit by itself—it's certainly among the five nicest restaurant exteriors in the Cities, counting the tragically closed Town Talk Diner in Longfellow, Minneapolis.

Rustica, 816 W. 46th St., Minneapolis, MN 55409; (612) 822-1119; rusticabakery.com; Bakery; $$. Make no bones about it: If you want the best baguette in the Twin Cities (and possibly the country), Rustica has it. It's a baguette so good that natives of France have been known to try it and declare it edible—a crispy, chewy exterior, a substantial crumb with real flavor that invites the application of homemade jam or golden, creamery-fresh butter, or a drizzle of olive oil and sea salt. Available at various grocery store outlets (including **Seward Co-op,** p. 218), the Rustica baguette is the baton of excellence against which other breads are measured and inevitably found to be at least a little bit lacking. Rustica's other baked goods are well liked, too—they make a bittersweet chocolate cookie that gets local food-lovers seriously hot and bothered, and chewy chocolate-chip-style cookies that are equally tasty. All in all, if you're going to go out of your way to patronize a Minneapolis or St. Paul bakery, this is a good starting place (although **Patisserie 46,** p. 106, and **Salty Tart,** p. 122, have their share of partisans, as well, and doughnuts are a whole 'nother dimension.)

Rye Deli, 1930 Hennepin Ave., Minneapolis, MN 55403; (612) 871-1200; ryedeli.com; Deli; $$. This "Montreal style" deli ("smoked meat" instead of pastrami, and thick-cut corned beef) set off a firestorm of controversy when it debuted in 2011, as deli hardliners declared it either delicious or not up to snuff. What seems clear after a couple visits is that it's a clean, modern, good-looking establishment that serves fine ingredients in a variety of traditional ways, albeit in a manner that won't put NYC on the defensive. Whether the end product is truly deli or not will depend a lot on your background, your place of birth, and how much of a hardliner you are for a particular style or cut of meat. Still, for a late-night nosh, it's a nice alternative to the Uptown wall of sushi.

Safari Express, 920 E. Lake St. # 134, Minneapolis, MN 55407; (612) 874-0756; safariexpresstogo.com; Somali; $. Home to the famous and remarkably good camel burger, Safari Express in the Midtown Global Market is the tip of what many hope is an iceberg of second-generation Somali and Ethiopian restaurants that have a foot planted firmly in the homeland while also catering to the palates and expectations of fourth- and fifth-generation Minnesotans. The lean, juicy camel burger comes on a buttered bun with lettuce, tomato, and red onion, plus cheese and its appealingly earthy flavor is nicely offset by an accompanying slice of pineapple.

Saffron Restaurant & Lounge, 123 N. 3rd St., Minneapolis, MN 55401; (612) 746-5533; saffronmpls.com; Middle Eastern; $$$. Saffron is a rare downtown dynamo—it straddles the worlds of pre-club grub and haute cuisine with ease. The restaurant is helmed by 20-something Chef Sameh Wadi, who, at age 25, was the youngest chef ever to compete as a contestant on Food Network's *Iron Chef*. Wadi and his avuncular brother Saed (who handles the front of the house) have built a miniature empire that sprouted from their Mediterranean roots: the tapas-style Middle Eastern and North African small plates of Saffron, the eclectic food truck World Street Kitchen, and a line of house-ground spices called Spice Trail. Saffron's atmosphere is sleek but approachable, and the menu has enough variety—from small tastes to big plates like a melt-in-your-mouth lamb tagine—that most groups and tastes can be accommodated. No pork products are served in-house, so it's a kosher- and halal-friendly destination for diners. The presence of dishes like lamb bacon and *bistirma* (an air-cured beef equivalent to prosciutto) means that even pork-a-philes will walk away satisfied. See Chef Wadi's recipe for **Spiced Lamb & Mejdool Date Tagine** on page 241.

Saigon Uptown Restaurant, 3035 Lyndale Ave. South, Minneapolis, MN 55408; (612) 827-8918; Chinese and Vietnamese; $$. This venerable hole-in-the-wall has built up a loyal following for its soulful, massive, dirt-cheap pho, one of the world's finest tools for surviving a northern winter. While the ambiance is sparse, to be charitable, if you're going to Saigon, you're going for the big bowls of soup, not the interior decorating. You probably shouldn't go for the service, either; it can take a while.

Salty Tart, 920 E. Lake St., Minneapolis, MN 55407; (612) 874-9206; saltytart.com; Bakery; $$. Beard-nominated and *Bon Appétit*-celebrated baker Michelle Gayer is rightfully known citywide for the quality of her product, which is up there with the likes of **Patisserie 46** (p. 106) and **Rustica Bakery** (p. 119) in terms of its sophistication, consistency, and overall flavor. Visitors to Gayer's charming bakery counter in the bustling and polyglot Midtown Global Market can choose from sweet (like rustic fruit tarts), savory (like ham sandwiches and croissants), and super-sweet (like surprisingly light and delicate chocolate cupcakes with Surly beer-infused frosting and crunchy little dark chocolate pearls on top). A variety of other tastes (baguettes, macarons, cobbler, etc.) come and go with the seasons and whims of Gayer, but the place is always reliable for a sugar and pastry–based pick-me-up.

Sample Room, 2124 Marshall St. Northeast, Minneapolis, MN 55418; (612) 789-0333; the-sample-room.com; New American; $$. When the Sample Room opened in 2002, it was a dazzling new concept: eclectic small plates with an emphasis on cheese and meat, evocative of Spanish tapas but adapted to local food. As the years have gone by, the Sample Room has kept its knives sharp and its ideas fresh—while the essential concept remains, there's a lot of invention and reinvention going on in the menu, and its joyful pursuit of good food is evident to guests who glance at its small but well curated menu. The restaurant wears its ambition on its sleeve—in 2011, Chef Matt Paulson embarked on a project to make 100 different sorts of sausages in-house, keeping notes along the way. Moody, chic, and comfortable, the Sample Room is a cocktail bar as much as a restaurant and is a fine place for a late-night belt, a small snack, or a full-on meal, as the mood suits you.

Sanctuary, 903 Washington Ave. South, Minneapolis, MN 55415; (612) 339-5058; sanctuaryminneapolis.com; Fusion; $$$. A posh, eclectic, intimate spot near Downtown, Sanctuary presents a fresh, vibrant, sometimes twisted gastronomic sensibility brought to Minneapolis via the edgy port city of Marseilles, France, hometown to Chef Patrick Atanalian. Influences are constantly shifting and mixing—that might mean escargot and andouille on a bagel with shiitake mushrooms, or pan-seared duck breast on a waffle with a sweet onion coffee liqueur marmalade. If there's any underlining backbone to the restaurant's offerings, it's Chef Atanalian's French influence, but sometimes the riffs get so wild and inspired that you have to hunt to find it. Constantly shifting seasonal and special dinner menus add even more excitement to the mix—this place is about as far from Applebee's as you can get, and it's got the gargoyle-themed decor to prove it.

Sapor Cafe and Bar, 428 Washington Ave. North, Minneapolis, MN 55401; (612) 375-1971; saporcafe.com; Fusion; $$. This over-looked little gem in Minneapolis's warehouse district is a favorite of locals, who savor its reasonably priced fusion offerings, bright flavors, and cozy atmosphere. A single meal might have a diner bouncing from the bayou to China to Central America and back by way of Wisconsin cheese, but that's part of the charm of the place. Sapor has taken advantage of Minnesota's sometimes arctic climate by establishing itself as one of the city's leading destinations for hot soup—the selection changes daily.

Sawatdee, 607 Washington Ave. South, #100, Minneapolis, MN 55415; (612) 338-6451; plus numerous other locations in the Cities; Thai; $$. Sawatdee is the baseline for Thai food in the Twin Cities and its influence is wide-reaching—its flavors are calm and approachable, its decor rich with old-fashioned Thai charm, and its service and product consistent. You won't push any cultural or gastronomic boundaries here, but you will have a comfortable Thai meal that will please a Midwestern palate.

Sea Change Restaurant & Bar, 806 S. 2nd St., Minneapolis, MN 55415; (612) 225-6499; seachangempls.com; Seafood; $$$. You wouldn't think that Minneapolis or St. Paul would be particularly hot on seafood, and generally you'd be right. Sea Change is one of the standout exceptions to that reasonable assumption—dedicated to sustainable seafood and attached to the thriving Guthrie Theater in downtown, Sea Change has the robust (and well-heeled) customer base necessary to demand and obtain good fish. For lunch the dining room feels semi-empty and a bit corporate, but when the restaurant fills up at night (particularly on evenings featuring a well-attended play), it lights up and is as lively a nightspot as you're likely to find downtown. Fronted by heavy hitter Tim McKee, Sea Change is gastronomically dependable and admirably dedicated to giving diners a nice price range to choose from—one can assemble an eclectic small plates meal or go big and nosh on the likes of barramundi or duck.

Sen Yai Sen Lek, 2422 Central Ave. Northeast, Minneapolis, MN 55418; (612) 781-3046; senyai-senlek.com; Thai; $$. Literally "big noodle, little noodle," Sen Yai Sen Lek takes Thai cuisine and marries it to the seasonal and local food movements, creating a menu that applies Thai flavor balance and passion to whatever happens to be in season and/or exciting to Chef-Owner Joe Hatch-Surisook. By balancing the flavors of salty, sweet, sour, bitter, spicy, and "neutral," Hatch-Surisook has managed to create a notable stop for diners from around the area in search of a new twist on Asian favorites. In addition to familiar curries and noodle dishes, Sen Yai Sen Lek offers a number of Isaan sticky rice entree options that may pleasantly push the boundaries of diners unused to venturing past pad Thai and pineapple curry.

Seven Sushi Steakhouse, Ultralounge and Skybar, 700 Hennepin Ave., Minneapolis, MN 55403; (612) 238-7770; 7mpls.com; Steak House; $$$. The downtown business set likes to live large, and

that's the sort of thing that Seven does well—from bottle service to (workmanlike) sushi to steak to big, beefy portions of pasta to seafood towers, there's not a big appetite it can't meet. It also fulfills another popular downtown request: an ambitious rooftop patio with bar and dining area, locally known for its happy hour.

Solera, 900 Hennepin Ave., Minneapolis, MN 55403; (612) 338-0062; solera-restaurant.com; Spanish; $$$. Spanish food is generally a non-presence in the Twin Cities area, but Solera does its best to represent the gastronomic treasures of Spain. From its *Jamon Iberico de Bellota* (the famous and extremely pricey ham beloved by Spaniards) to charcuterie, chorizo, Spanish cheeses, paella, and a wide range of tapas, Solera runs the gamut of southern Spanish classics. Depending on the night of the week and the event or events being hosted, Solera can feel like a cozy local eatery, or a sprawling, multitiered nightclub that just happens to also sell tapas—guests visiting on the weekends are advised to make reservations and brace themselves for a zesty night on the town. When the weather's warm, Solera often plays movies on its rooftop, one of the most popular open-air gathering places for downtown Minneapolitans.

Sonora Grill, 920 E. Lake St., Minneapolis, MN 55407; (612) 871-1900; midtownglobalmarket.org/SonoraGrill; Mexican; $$. Newly founded Sonora Grill at the Midtown Global Market takes the fine-dining training of founding partner Alejandro Castillon and channels it into a seemingly unusual direction: Mexican street food. The result is a casual counter-style eatery that dishes up impeccably prepared and plated soul food classics such as skewered meat called *pinchos*, small sandwiches called *bocadillos*, and cheesy tacos called *caramelos*. Visitors should also consider Sonora Grill for a casual but hearty Mexican breakfast—its breakfast burrito and *chilaquiles* are long on both charm and flavor. And while the place draws much of its inspiration from just below the US-Mexico border, its chimichurri hails from even farther south—Argentina.

Sopranos Italian Kitchen, 5331 W. 16th St., Minneapolis, MN 55416; (952) 345-2400; sopranosmn.com; Italian; $$$. An inauspiciously named Italian eatery in the newly developing West End section of town (if anyone gets to name an Italian restaurant "Sopranos," it should be HBO and/or David Chase), Sopranos has a polished slickness that suggests customers paying a lot of money for food poured out of plastic bags onto expensive plates. Happily, that's not the case—the impeccably groomed and business-friendly exterior conceals the beating heart of a real restaurant, where simple dishes like a sausage and peppers starter and the old standard of spaghetti and meatballs really shine on the strength of good balance, serious ingredients, and a level of care in the kitchen that translates well to the plate. With restaurants like **Broders'** (p. 19) in Minneapolis proper, it's hard to make a case for Sopranos as a destination spot, but if you're nearby, it's a satisfying meal amid lovely decor served by warm, well-trained servers.

Stub & Herb's Restaurant & Bar, 227 SE Oak St., Minneapolis, MN 55455; (612) 379-0555; stubandherbsbar.com; Pub; $$. This dimly lit, convivial, and otherwise unremarkable campus beer and burger bar made a big push into craft beer in the late '00s, with spectacular results—its tables and barstools quickly filled with members of the burgeoning local craft beer community, who clamored for the extensive draught list of locally made artisan beers, seasonal draughts suited to the weather, and new releases of the hottest beers being put onto the local market. It's now the place on campus to go for beer events and new releases, and its dozens of draught lines are put to good used showing off the latest works of brewhouses such as Summit, Surly, Schell's, Lift Bridge, Wisconsin's Tyranena, and more.

Sun Street Breads, 4600 Nicollet Ave., Suite A, Minneapolis, MN 55419; (612) 354-3414; sunSt.breads.com; Bakery; $$. Founded by baker Solveig (literally "Sun Street" in Norwegian) Tofte, Sun Street combines careful scratch baking with casual noshes—biscuit-sandwich driven breakfasts, hearty sandwiches including one of the best meat loaf dishes in town (served with apple butter and fried shallot cream cheese), and hearty, simple, smart dishes that take good approachable ingredients and combine them with clever twists like stew served on hominy with corn bread with pepper jelly or beef pasty with a carrot-onion marmalade. Tofte's passion for baking is matched by her experience (she hails from the Turtle bread mini-empire, among other places), and her skills shine through in the quality of her baked goods.

Surdyk's Flights, Minneapolis Airport, Terminal 1 (Lindbergh), Minneapolis, MN 55111; surdyksflights.com; New American; $$. Airports nationwide (and to some extent, worldwide) have historically been culinary black holes. Travelers at the mercy of airline timetables tend to wildly overpay for the worst-quality comfort food, grudgingly prepared by workers left grumpy by the daily commute into a highly secure location. The antidote is newly established restaurants that prepare thoughtful food with care—Surdyk's Flights certainly is prominent among their ranks in Minneapolis-St. Paul, offering wine flights, panini, cheese plates, house-made pretzels, and dishes such as salmon in parchment and a prosciutto and pecorino sandwich featuring meat made by Iowa's nationally renowned La Quercia. The shop's "buy and fly" program lets visitors bring properly packaged food (or bottled wine) onto their flights, making for a considerably more pleasant voyage.

Sushi Tango, 3001 Hennepin Ave. #F201, Minneapolis, MN 55408; (612) 822-7787 sushitango.com; Japanese; $$. The natural sushi companion to the bro bars that liberally dot Uptown, Sushi Tango is a clubby, convivial, playful restaurant that takes sushi out of its rarefied haute cuisine element and plunks it firmly down into the center of the Friday night party scene. While the menu does get past rolls and nigiri into some hibachi favorites, it's a step behind *izakaya* spots like the nearby **Moto-i** (p. 99). Its happy hour, however, is one of the best standing local deals for those hoping to snag California rolls on the cheap. **Additional location:** 8362 Tamarack Village, Woodbury, MN 55125; (651) 578-0064.

Taco Taxi, 1511 E. Lake St., Minneapolis, MN 55407; (612) 722-3293; tacotaximn.com; Mexican; $. Cheap prices, late hours, and tacos stuffed to the bursting point with spicy, moist meat and balanced with onions, lime, and cilantro in true street taco style—it's hard to beat Taco Taxi for a divey street food experience in Minneapolis. Born from the food traditions of Jalisco, Mexico, Taco Taxi also takes its product to the street in its food truck incarnation, which pops up at neighborhood festivals and art fairs throughout the city. Carne asada and al pastor tacos are approachable and delicious, but try the *tripa* (tripe, or intestines) if you dare—it's a house favorite.

Taqueria La Hacienda, 334 E. Lake St. #101, Minneapolis, MN 55408; (612) 822-2715; taqueriaslahacienda.com/home-english .htm; Mexican; $. Taqueria La Hacienda sells plenty of things other than tacos al pastor, but I wouldn't know—these crispy, flavor-rich little bits of pork served on corn tortillas with onions, cilantro, and lime juice are some of the tastiest bites of food—of any kind—available in the Twin Cities, and a full order of three is less than $10. Casual but comfortable ambiance and a diverse clientele for the East Lake locations in particular mean that Taqueria La Hacienda is a nice way to step into the working-class cosmopolitan vibe that defines South Minneapolis. **Additional locations:** 1515 E. Lake St., #104, Minneapolis, MN 55407; (612) 728-5424; 2000 Williams Dr., #105, Burnsville, MN 55337; (952) 808-6895.

Tea House, 2425 University Ave. Southeast, Minneapolis, MN 55414; (612) 331-8866; ourteahouse.com; Chinese; $$. Spicy Szechuan favorites tempered with gentle Chinese-American classics make this popular local Chinese chain (often named local Best of) a no-brainer destination for an Asian-inflected nosh. Clean simple flavors win over many diners, and the menu style is well suited toward big groups sharing numerous entrees, assisted by a lazy Susan. Despite the name, don't come for the tea—selection is quite limited, and prices high. **Additional locations:** 88 Nathan Lane, Plymouth, MN 55441; (763) 544-3422; 1676 Suburban Ave., St. Paul, MN 55106; (651) 771-1790; 2nd Floor of The Towle Building; 330 S. 2nd Ave., Minneapolis, MN 55401; (612) 343-2133.

Ted Cook's 19th Hole, 2814 E. 38th St., Minneapolis, MN 55406; (612) 721-2023; tedcooks19thholebbq.com; Barbecue; $$. Ted Cook's is an old-school barbecue place in the best and worst senses of the phrase. The takeout-only restaurant's decor is dingy (although a newly painted and artfully done mural on the exterior helps distract from that), the potato jojos are inevitably soggy, and the restaurant's second-class meat can wander toward fatty. It'll also come drenched in sauce unless you think to order your entrees dry. But deep, smoky flavor is a constant, there are typically no unpleasantly gelatinous "fall off the bone" ribs to worry about, and the sweet potato pie sold for dessert is second to none.

Tilia, 2726 W. 43rd St., Minneapolis, MN 55410; (612) 354-2806; tiliampls.com; New American; $$$. Along with **Travail** (p. 43), **Patisserie 46** (p. 106), and **Pizzeria Lola** (p. 111), Tilia is one of the breakthrough, blockbuster, lines-around-the-block places to open in recent years in Minneapolis, making the southwest part of the city the unexpected place to be for hot new high-end dining destinations. (**In Season,** p. 85, hasn't been as mobbed, but it deserves a mention in this context, as well.) Tilia's the creation of big-deal Steven Brown, who draws his own bold-faced ink on the strength of his cooking style, which is bold, direct, balanced, and invigorating. You'll find that Tilia, if you can get a table (there are no reservations here), is a place that puts food first, with top-notch ingredients being used in smart, simple ways that highlight their natural advantages. It's also a great spot to take kids—the kids' menu is smart and fun, and shows a level of thought unusual for a restaurant with fine-dining chops. Don't miss brunch, which is easily one of the best in the Cities.

Tin Fish, 3000 Calhoun Pkwy. East, Minneapolis, MN 55408; (612) 823-5840; thetinfish.net/LC-MN/index.htm; Seafood; $$. The far-sighted planning of a series of Minneapolis civic leaders and mayors (including a mayor who would later become vice president, Hubert Humphrey) led to the creation of an extensive series of parks and walking paths around Minneapolis area lakes, making the city one of the most walkable, bikeable, and generally enjoyable in the country (particularly during the warmer months). Paradoxically, the protected status of the city's lakes and rivers means that it's quite difficult to open businesses of any sort with a view of the water, making Tin Fish at Lake Calhoun one of the few games in town (see also **Sea Salt**, p. 40, and **Bread & Pickle**, p. 57). Part of a national chain, the Tin Fish enjoys a prime location by the water, dispensing relatively expensive fish sandwiches, soups, and fish tacos of adequate quality. It's a spot well worth enjoying for the view and the gorgeous summertime lakeside dining, although "dining" may be too generous a word for the scarfing of fried fish on metal picnic tables.

Tracy's Saloon and Eatery, 2207 E. Franklin Ave., Minneapolis, MN 55404; (612) 332-1865; tracyssaloon.com; Pub; $$. Beaten-up black vinyl and old carpeting mark this place as a dive, but if you dig into Tracy's Saloon and Eatery, there's a story to discover. The place exists as a tenuous compromise between the holdovers from the old Tracy's Saloon (burgers and beer, mostly) and the new, sometimes gastronomically daring Eatery, which includes items like pan-fried Wisconsin rainbow trout and apple-cured ribs with dipping sauce. Quality beer (including local favorites like Surly and Summit) has pushed its way into taps that used to have only the likes of Grain Belt Premium and Miller Lite, and its new owners (who took over in 2006) have gone to great lengths to make sure that the place remains both a neighborhood hub and a beacon to those in search of a pub-grub adventure.

Trattoria Tosca, 3415 W. 44th St., Minneapolis, MN; 55410; (612) 924-1900; trattoriatosca.com; Italian, $$$. There's no reason why Trattoria Tosca should feel like a secret—it's in a popular, well-heeled neighborhood, and its food and service are remarkably polished and consistent. And yet it's a quiet, eminently civilized, rarely a bustle romantic spot convenient to South Minneapolis and Edina, dishing up sophisticated pasta entrees for a largely neighborhood crowd. From a food consistency perspective, Tosca shines—it's one of those rare places where you can tell a would-be diner—"get whatever looks good; it will be." While a bit spendy, your money gets you a comfortable upscale atmosphere, well-trained servers, and spot-on eats—a fair exchange.

True Thai, 2627 E. Franklin Ave., Minneapolis, MN 55406; (612) 375-9942; truethairestaurant.com; Thai; $$. Fronted by flamboyant dynamo Anna Prasomphol Fieser and dedicated to faithfully re-creating Thai flavor profiles in the arctic wilds of Minnesota, True Thai makes regular appearances on local "best of" lists for its consistent, passionate execution of southeast Asian classics. This Seward neighborhood anchor expanded into a next-door space in 2010 and now offers multiple expansive dining rooms in addition to its bustling take-out business. The bright, deeply spiced flavors of its curries are a constant, but guests seeking heat should speak up—like most Thai restaurants in the Cities, the chili heat level of dishes has been adapted to work with the reigning mild palate of the Scandinavian/Germanic natives.

Turtle Bread Co., 4762 Chicago Ave., Minneapolis, MN 55407; (612) 823-7333; turtlebread.com; Bakery; $$. This simple bakery gone upscale concept serves comforting classics (croissants, cakes, hearth breads, Danishes, house-made pies) and straightforward but nicely executed classic breakfasts such as eggs Benedict with a slice of house-made baguette and jam. Food choices vary from location to location—Chicago Avenue is attached to **Cafe Levain** (p. 61), and Pizza Biga, Linden Hills is side by side with the stellar

Trattoria Tosca (p. 134), and Longfellow stands alone with breakfast and a soup-salad-sandwich-driven lunch service that may soon expand to dinner. The atmosphere in all locations is upscale without being stuffy or smothering, favoring lots of natural light and big comfortable wooden tables. **Additional locations:** 3421 W. 44th St., Minneapolis, MN 55410; (612) 924-6013; 4205 E. 34th St., Minneapolis, MN 55406; (612) 545-5757.

Uncle Franky's, 728 Broadway St. Northeast, Minneapolis, MN 55413; (612) 455-2181; unclefrankys.com; Hot Dogs; $. Hot dogs tend to get overlooked, and that's a shame—a good dog is far more than a snack, it's a perfect American sausage, it's a soft but character-rich bakery-made bun, and it's a constellation of good toppings applied in a balanced way. Few restaurants (and this even includes a number of hot dog–only restaurants) understand this, but Uncle Franky's nails it. Home to what is likely the area's best Chicago dog (a beautiful creature capable of giving Chicago-born

Chicago dogs a good run for their money), Uncle Franky's combines a hectic, college-student-friendly atmosphere with good quick eats to make an ideal filling station for the dude or lady on the go. Far from fine dining, but a nice bite of local flair—and the price is right, too. **Additional locations:** 10160 6th Ave. North, Plymouth, MN 55441; (763) 746-3643; 1316 4th St. Southeast, Dinkydale Arcade, Minneapolis, MN; (612) 379-5589.

Victor's 1959 Cafe, 3756 Grand Ave. South, Minneapolis, MN 55409; (612) 827-8948; victors1959cafe.com; Cuban; $$. Open for more than a decade and by now a well-loved neighborhood rallying place, Victor's 1959 Cafe is thick with Cuban-revolution-inspired atmosphere and homey, savory food that revolves around the staples of Latin America and the Caribbean. Graffiti-bedecked walls, mural-splashed tables, and eye-poppingly colorful wall art make Victor's a feast for the senses, and the lively vibe of the place carries over into the food, which includes everything from marinated strip steak to Creole shrimp to mango salmon, generally swimming in some combination of sides including *tostones*, fried sweet plantains, and/or beans and rice. Victor's does one of the most distinctive brunches in the Cities, dishing up big scramblers and a tasty mango waffle with Creole/Latin flair. The list of sides is as long as the menu, allowing guests to pick and choose their way to the Cuban-style brunch of their dreams.

Victory 44 and Victory 44 Coffee Bar and Provisions, 2201 N. 44th Ave., Minneapolis, MN 55412; (612) 588-2228;

victory-44.com; New American; $$$. This singularly interesting North Minneapolis fine-dining spot is one of the few spots (see also: **Travail,** p. 43, founded by Victory 44 alums, and **Heidi's,** p. 82) to do molecular gastronomy, using science to push the boundaries of dining. An ever-changing blackboard posts the shockingly reasonable prices of dishes featuring ingredients as encouraging as rabbit porchetta or torchon of *foie gras*, or as daunting as tongue or bone marrow. The chefs are also the servers, so be prepared for a more rough-and-tumble—but often thoroughly charming—experience made particularly special by the creative and adventurous nature of the cuisine being served. The Perfect Burger is a dish that many locals would say lives up to its name. Dogwood Coffee and elegant but satisfying breakfast entrees (soft eggs and maple sausage, waffles du jour) make the next-door coffee bar a joy to visit.

The Wienery, 414 Cedar Ave. South, Minneapolis, MN 55454; (612) 333-5798; wienery.com; Hot Dogs and Breakfast; $. There are restaurants out there that work to avoid being seen as gritty, or working class, or "divey," frantically trying to impress diners with spotless surfaces and a suburban-ready facade. Not the Wienery, which hangs prison ID bracelets up behind its grimy counter and practically dares you to call the health department when you walk in the door. The faint of heart will walk back out. The wise and courageous will order a hot dog or three—while the decor is grubby, the grub is great. The shop's deluxe Vienna beef dogs feature well-balanced mixes of toppings, breakfast items are hearty, classic American standards done competently, and there's an extensive palate of vegetarian and vegan options, too.

Wilde Roast Cafe, 65 SE Main St., Minneapolis, MN 55414; (612) 331-4544; wilderoastcafe.com; Cafe; $$. More than a cafe but a bit less than a restaurant (perhaps the term "gastro-cafe" was invented for places like this and **Muddy Waters,** p. 100, in Uptown), the Wilde Roast is an unusual, multipurpose beast, host to everyone from studying students to dining grown-ups and random passersby who just duck in for a cup of coffee (or gelato, in summertime). The cafe does a hearty full breakfast service with a luxe brunch add-on on the weekends until mid-afternoon, and while its stock in trade is coffee drinks, plenty of folks frequent the cafe for its sandwiches, wraps, and flatbread pizzas. The feel of Wilde Roast is civilized and urban, with plenty of space between tables and plenty of room to spread out and feel comfortable. There's also a small event space near the back of the cafe that can be used for meetings and presentations (inquire for details).

Wise Acre Eatery, 5401 Nicollet Ave. South, Minneapolis, MN 55419; (612) 354-2577; wiseacreeatery.com; Farm-to-Table; $$. Founded by well-credentialed culinary refugees from the venerable Lucia's franchise (which is headed in turn by Twin Cities slow food pioneer Lucia Watson), Wise Acre Eatery represents an attempt to bring farm-to-table to a neighborhood audience without losing its luster. The farm-to-table thing is no joke at Wise Acre; as per the menu: "Tangletown Gardens' Farm, a 100+ acre farm located outside of Plato, MN, supplies the farm-raised produce as well as raises Scottish Highland cattle and Berkshire Hogs for Wise Acre meat, and chickens for both meat and eggs." The attempt to bring high-end local eats into a neighborhood bistro setting yields mixed results: Portions are small and expensive, but quality tends to be high and flavors bright. Its frozen custard (a holdover from previous building occupant Liberty Frozen Custard) lacks the rich smoothness that the dessert is capable of, but its pork dishes and soups tend to be stellar. If they're serving fried chicken, try it—they've got a deft touch with the dish. And the house-made nonalcoholic beverages are sophisticated, more like a sleek, mixologist-made cocktail in terms of flavor profile than a fountain soda.

Wok in the Park, 3005 Utah Ave., St. Louis Park, MN 55426; (952) 657-5754; wokintheparkrestaurant.com; Asian; $$. An MSG-free fresh Asian bistro that takes classic Chinese and Thai comfort food into the 21st century, Wok in the Park is one of those happy places that manages to take dishes you know and love and freshen them up without losing their essence. Little touches (scallions in the crab rangoon, simple Westernized names for the various soups, inspired conch fritters served with homemade ranch dressing) make the menu both entertaining and accessible, and while the food is simple, it's not dumbed down. The clean, undivided dining room can get a bit raucous on busy nights, so it's fine "dining with the dudes and/or ladies" destination, but less ideal for a romantic evening.

YoYo Donuts & Coffee Bar, 5757 Sanibel Dr., Minnetonka, MN 55343; (952) 960-1800; yoyodonuts.com; Bakery; $. The bacon-maple long john—dressed up with a real strip of bacon across the top of the doughnut—has become the unofficial calling card of YoYo Donuts, a newly opened fancy-pants doughnut shop in Minnetonka. The doughnut craze hit the Twin Cities hard in 2010–11, with the dawning realization that many of the old standbys were no longer cutting it, and that a more creative approach could be taken to the breakfast pastries our fathers and mothers (and grandfathers and grandmothers) grew up munching on to start their days. The scratch baking of YoYo includes cake doughnuts, yeast-raised doughnuts, and specialty pastries including apple fritters, maple-glazed cinnamon rolls and hot caramel rolls, and the aforementioned bacon-maple long john. The coffee at YoYo is good enough to suit its raised and glazed companions—it's managed by Dogwood Coffee Company, one of the area's leading third-wave providers of fine coffee.

St. Paul & Suburbs

St. Paul is very much a city on the grow. In the past decade, its restaurant and bar scene has blossomed, and between street food and some thoughtful high-end places in downtown and lowertown, the quieter of the two Twins has certainly hit its stride. There are old, charming ethnic places a plenty (Italian and German in particular), but if you're looking for craft beer, first-rate bakeries, or farm-to-table dining, this newly spunky state capital can be of service. And those hoping to do a stroll (food focused or otherwise) should consider hitting Grand Avenue, an eminently walkable stretch of turf west of St. Paul's downtown.

St. Paul Landmarks

Cafe Latte, 850 Grand Ave., St. Paul, MN 55105; (651) 224-5687; cafelatte.com; Downtown St. Paul, 7th St. & Grand Ave.; Cafe and Bakery; $$. St. Paul's Cafe Latte has assumed a grand reputation locally for its desserts, but choose wisely—while there are often 15 to 20 different selections on offer over the course of a given day, some will be excellent, some good, and some merely tolerable. The almond coffee cake is a home run, as is the shop's lemon torte. Regardless of how you fare at dessert roulette, you'll likely enjoy the restaurant's stylish and expansive seating area and coffee selection as you sit, sip, and munch—it's a favorite spot for locals to meet, do business, and people watch on Grand Avenue. The restaurant also offers soups, salads, sandwiches, breads, scones, pizza, and wine, all of which are satisfactory and reasonably priced, particularly considering the posh neighborhood surroundings.

Cecil's Deli, 651 Cleveland Ave. South, St. Paul, MN 55116; (651) 698-0334; cecilsdeli.com; Deli; $$. Jewish delis are few

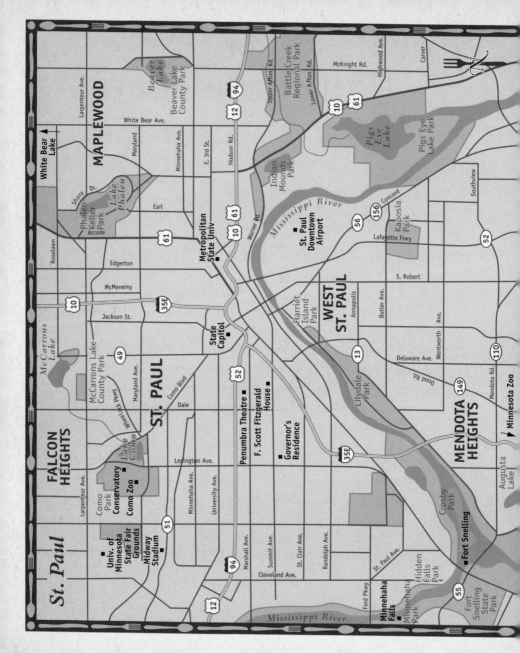

and far between in this land of frosty blond giants, but Cecil's comes through with a simple, traditional approach to the form. Favorites like bagels, *rugelach*, and *hamentashen* spill forth from the bakery, and the restaurant side of the operation is an earthy affair, serving up filling deli sandwiches and heavy, egg-and-potatoes–style breakfasts. The dining room wouldn't be out of place in New York, which is to say it's long on function, short on form. If you're a corned beef fan, this is a fine place to get your fix—they'll slice it thin for you, and you can bring it home with a nice loaf of egg white bread. Side note: If you're a mustard fan, Cecil's is your place—the small grocery store section of the deli sells several dozen varieties.

Dari-Ette Drive In, 1440 E. Minnehaha Ave., St. Paul, MN 55106; (651) 776-3470; facebook.com/pages/Dari-ette-Drive-In/; Diner; $. Fans of Italian-American food and old-school drive-in culture have met their match made in heaven with the Dari-Ette, a beaten-down but still lively spot east of downtown St. Paul in a traditionally Italian neighborhood that is slowly transforming into a Latino district. Best bets include the Hot Italiano sandwich (a politically correct hot dago sandwich, featuring spicy Italian sausage, marinara sauce, melted mozzarella cheese, and Italian bread) and the luscious fresh banana malt, a treat unique to the Dari-Ette. The drive-in sells its own spaghetti sauce by the pint, quart, and gallon, and also boasts a decent traditional drive-in burger, to boot. Good taste overpowers grit by at least 2-to-1, and the Dari-Ette's easily worth the trip for the blast of St. Paul neighborhood culture that it delivers.

DeGidio's Restaurant and Bar, 425 7th St. West, St. Paul, MN 55102; (651) 291-7105; degidios.com; Downtown St. Paul, 7th St. & Grand Ave.; Italian-American; $. Sometimes you want sophisticated Continental Italian, with its emphasis on fish, seasonal produce, and impeccably balanced regional specialties. And sometimes you want a mass of cheese and garlic bread and meatballs. When it's the latter sort of evening, DeGidio's Restaurant and Bar should be your first stop in St. Paul. This warm, old-school charmer is smaller than the better-known Cosetta's, and the food has more soul. Live like a local and get a hot dago sandwich, a sprawling open-faced mass of cheese, sauce, sausage, and bread that requires a fork and knife and will fill you up for a week should you dare to finish it. On a cold winter night, few Twin Cities specialties are as profoundly warming.

Glockenspiel, 605 7th St. West, St. Paul, MN 55102; (651) 292-9421; glockenspielrestaurant.com; Downtown St. Paul, 7th St. & Grand Ave.; German; $$. You can't accuse Martin Ziegler, the German-born owner of the Glockenspiel, of going halfway with his German theme: every item on the menu is titled in German, there's an accordion player on Friday and Saturday nights, and when Oktoberfest rolls around each year, the place reverberates with meat raffles, a "Name that Sausage" contest, and a sauerkraut-eating competition. The schnitzel, pork chops, and liver and onions are all

Booya!

In St. Paul, the longstanding Upper Midwestern tradition of **booya** (or booyah) lives on. Thought to be derived from the French language words for broth (bouillon) or "to boil" (bouillir), a booya is a massive stew made and then served communally, usually consisting of beef, vegetables, and a massive sachet of spices contained in a cheesecloth bag. The tradition has been traced in a slow migration west from northeastern Wisconsin; Green Bay is seen as its likely point of origin.

September and October are peak booya season, but they happen as early as June. One of the biggest is the Silver Fox Booya, held in the Highland Park neighborhood of St. Paul. A new tradition is the Jewish Community Center of the Greater St. Paul Area's "Booya in the Sukkah," which combines kosher booya with the Jewish fall harvest holiday of Sukkot. If you haven't eaten stew in an improvised outdoor religious shelter made of sticks and leaves, you haven't truly lived.

soulfully competent, but the sausages are the real draw: make sure you sample the Bratwürste, two boiled and seared sausages served with sauerkraut, bread, and mustard and available under the "Light Entrees" section of the menu. The atmosphere is no joke, either—from the fixtures to the knickknacks, the restaurant feels as though Bavaria itself waltzed into town and deposited an antiques store's worth of goodies before flying back to Europe.

Gopher Bar, 241 7th St. East, St. Paul, MN 55101; (651) 291-9638; gopherbar.com; Downtown St. Paul, 7th St. & Grand Ave.; Hot Dogs; $. Some restaurants should come with warning labels, and the Gopher Bar is one such place. Here's how it might read: "WARNING—Prepare to be offended." The Gopher Bar's slogan is "Sit Down, Shut Up, and Wait Your F***ing Turn," and the famously foul-mouthed staff take that attitude and run with it. Decor is abrasively right-wing (Obama fans may want to leave their pins at home), and the overall experience is something more appealing to the emotionally masochistic than, say, the typical American diner. All that said, the Coneys (Michigan-style loaded hot dogs with mustard, meat sauce, and onions) are outstanding and dirt cheap, and chances are, by the end of your meal, you'll have a story to tell your friends back home. Proceed with caution and a big appetite.

Heartland Restaurant and Farm Direct Market, 289 E. 5th St., St. Paul, MN 55101; (651) 699-3536; heartlandrestaurant.com; Downtown St. Paul, 7th St. & Grand Ave.; New American; $$$. There's no getting around the size of Chef Lenny Russo's ambition—Heartland is dedicated not just to being supremely locavore (it spurns olive oil in favor of locally made sunflower oil, for example) but also to being one of the highest-flying fine-dining experiences in the Twin Cities. Its massive, sleek, modern dining room delivers a top-flight dining experience and includes several private event spaces for catered events or tasting dinners, and the bar at Heartland has carved out its own formidable reputation by putting together craft cocktails that walk the line between classic flavors and cutting-edge infusions and micro-distilled spirits. Pork is a passion for Russo, and the restaurant has its own in-house charcuterie program under way, the two-year-plus cured results of which should be seeing the light of day any month now. For those who want to cook at home or gift to impress, Heartland's Farm Direct Market includes a small but thoughtfully curated selection of local jams and other value-added foods, including house-made pates, sausages, and other high-end craft foods produced with care and an eye toward highlighting Upper Midwestern purveyors and seasonality.

Izzy's Ice Cream Cafe, 2034 Marshall Ave., St. Paul, MN 55104; (651) 603-1458; izzysicecream.com; Ice Cream; $. The artisan ice cream of Izzy's has been attracting customers since 2000, and the shop's dedication to creative flavors and rich, velvet-textured product has helped the company grow steadily since its founding. Long, cheerful lines are a regular presence at the shop during summer months, and the Ice Cream Cafe also plays host to tours, ice cream-making parties that feature the creation of a new flavor that the group gets to design and name, and corporate events. On a high-tech note: The shop uses a radio frequency identification (RFID) system to keep customers updated on the 32 flavors available on a given day on an every-three-minute basis—the URL is flavorup.izzysicecream.com/flavor-grid, for those who want to flavor gawk.

Kopplin's Coffee, 2038 Marshall Ave., St. Paul, MN 55104; (651) 698-0457; kopplinscoffee.com; Coffee; $$. There are coffee-as-fuel people, coffee-as-craft people, and coffee-as-art people—the baristas at Kopplin's definitely fall into the last camp, making their beverages with all the care and fuss you'd associate with producing fine art. Although founder Andrew Kopplin is a relatively young guy for a standards-setting business owner, Kopplin's isn't for the coffee newbie—the discretion of the barista can and will override the discretion of the customer (good luck getting certain drinks to go, or with extra cream or sugar), but for those willing to wait, the experience, featuring top-of-the-line Clover equipment and detailed cupping notes, ranks up there with the best of the metro area's third wave generation of high-end coffee shops.

Mancini's Char House, 531 7th St. West, St. Paul, MN 55102; (651) 224-7345; mancinis.com; Steak House; $$$$. If you've ever wanted to hop into a time machine and have dinner at the sort of spot your grandparents probably frequented, your prayers have been answered: Mancini's Char House is an Italian-tinted old-fashioned steak house with a rowdy, cheery atmosphere, big-portioned meals focused on steaks and lobsters, open charcoal broilers, and generous antipasti plates. Stepping through the doors is like stepping backward in time, and part of that bargain is that you're willing to dine on an older schedule—meals can last a few hours, but those hours will fly as the drinks flow freely and your party enjoys a raucous conversation in the plush, cozy, enchantingly antique-feeling dining room.

Meritage, 410 Saint Peter St., St. Paul, MN 55102; (651) 222-5670; meritage-stpaul.com; Downtown St. Paul, 7th St. & Grand Ave.; French; $$$. Should you ever crave a serious cassoulet, Meritage is the place to come—its version of the French soul-food stew classic swims in rich, deep flavor and toothsome beans that play beautifully off the tender duck and pork confit that give it substance. The short, French-inspired menu here is a collection of no-brainers, essentially impossible to screw up—everything is hallowed classic done well, and served in a ritzy but not ponderous dining room of wood and mirrors. The newly added Meritage oyster bar works directly with oyster farms on both coasts to ensure a quality product, and it's one of the few places in the Cities one should be gulping down raw oysters with abandon. Don't miss the wild-caught Pacific shrimp cocktail with house-made sauce, either—it's a complete reboot of a formerly dead and useless menu item. The shrimp are meaty and brightly flavorful, the sauce zingy and natural tasting, rather than being mere spicy ketchup. Brunch is exceptional and should not be missed—be prepared to have fare such as steak and eggs with toast transformed through quality of ingredients, skill of preparation, and lots of butter into a shockingly pleasurable meal. See Chef Russell Klein's recipe for **Harvest Pumpkin Soup** on page 246.

Moscow on the Hill, 371 Selby Ave., St. Paul, MN 55102; (651) 291-1236; moscowonthehill.com; Russian; $$$. While it's not quite fair to the chefs of Moscow on the Hill to say that this Russian-themed eatery is best known for its vodka, this Russian-themed eatery is best known for its vodka. Special house infusions (including a horseradish vodka that is addictively delicious and charmingly sinus clearing) and six-shot flights of vodka will get you in trouble in a hurry, so designate a driver and pace yourself if you like good liquor. (And keep in mind that the flights are really more like six half-shots of vodka . . . which is still plenty for a lively meal.) Well-known dishes include blini and caviar, cured herring, meat-stuffed dumplings, and other such meaty, starchy, winter-friendly fare. The appetizers tend to be strong, but the quality of the entrees varies wildly, so diners may want to consider taking a vodka-themed happy hour here and then move on to another spot for dinner.

The Nook, 492 Hamline Ave. South, St. Paul, MN 55116; (651) 698-4347; crnook.com; American; $. So, you want to eat local? This is as local as it gets: a neighborhood-focused, local sports hero–themed burger bar that specializes in the Jucy Lucy, the cheese-stuffed hamburger that was born in South Minneapolis but perfected in St. Paul (see "Meat the Locals," pg. 196). While some of the South Minneapolis originators go in for low-grade burgers and straight-from-the-freezer fries, The Nook produces a beautiful, rich-tasting, well-balanced burger stuffed with decent American cheese and fresh-cut fries to rival any others in the Cities. And the beauty of the Jucy Lucy is that when the molten-hot cheese inevitably drips out of the center of your burger, it'll hit your fries and turn them into cheese fries. If you're getting dinner here, make sure you go early, or have a decent tolerance for waiting in line: as the name suggests, The Nook isn't huge and it fills up fast.

Phil's Tara Hideaway, 15021 60th St. North, Stillwater, MN 55082; (651) 439-9850; tarahideaway.com; Greek and American; $$$. An off-the-beaten-path restaurant with bootlegging roots, Phil's Tara Hideaway has layers like an onion: reputed gangster hideout, steak house, diner, Greek restaurant, modern fusion oasis. The cabin-like decor belies a sophisticated menu that marries the Greek background of owner Phil Barbatsis (as is reflected by Mediterranean meze plates and grilled octopus) with modern dishes prepared *sous vide* or with wild mushrooms. The menu's long enough to get lost in, so be prepared for a journey when you walk through the door.

Russian Piroshki & Tea House, 1758 University Ave. W, St. Paul, MN 55104; (651) 646-4144; Russian; $$. Should you find yourself tempted to explore this light-and-airy (but sometimes empty) light-hardwood-clad upstairs dining space, you'll have to do some planning. To sample the Tea House's simple menu of *piroshki* (aka "Russian hamburgers," much like pasties but filled with rice as well as ground beef), borscht, or beef stroganoff on dumplings, you'll have to come for lunch, and only on Wednesday through Saturday.

And to complicate things further, the stroganoff is only made on Friday. That said, it's a thoroughly charming and offbeat experience, like no other in the Twin Cities, and few others outside of, perhaps, Coney Island or Russia itself. The soulful simplicity of the food, the low prices, and the tea house charm of the photograph-bedecked upstairs dining space make this a one-of-a-kind gastro adventure in the Cities.

Tavern On Grand, 656 Grand Ave., St. Paul, MN 55105; (651) 228-9030; tavernongrand.com; Downtown St. Paul, 7th St. & Grand Ave.; American; $$. Known first and foremost for its walleye sandwich, Tavern on Grand is a bit of a contradiction—it's a log cabin–themed restaurant located in the heart of one of St. Paul's ritziest commercial strolls. The food is down-home, with an emphasis on burgers and classic sandwiches (steak, BLT, club, and so forth) with a bit of a North Woods salute in terms of the way items are named and otherwise presented on the menu. The walleye is the star, however, and it comes every which way from fried to roasted to grilled to served up ceviche style. Just don't ask if the walleye is local—like almost all the walleye served commercially in Minnesota, the fish hails from Canada.

St. Paul
Foodie Faves

Abu Nader Deli & Grocery, 2095 Como Ave., St. Paul, MN 55108; (651) 647-5391; Middle Eastern; $$. Fresh pita bread, Turkish coffee, and authentic-tasting, creamy-on-the-inside falafel are all charms of the humble but lovable Abu Nader Deli & Grocery in St. Paul. A few tables are available for those who would like to eat their Middle East food on the premises, and the rest of the small shop is dedicated to a specialty grocery store selling a small assortment of Middle Eastern wares (both **Bill's Imported Foods,** p. 179, and **Holy Land Bakery,** p. 181, are better destinations for those serious about shopping). That said, even with the spartan atmosphere, Abu Nader is a chow-hunter's delight.

Babani's Kurdish Restaurant, 544 Saint Peter St., St. Paul, MN 55102; (651) 602-9964; babanis.com; Downtown St. Paul, 7th St. &

Grand Ave.; Kurdish; $. There's not a lot of Kurdish food in the Twin Cities, but it's fair to say it's all good—Babani's Kurdish Restaurant is pretty much it, and it represents its home region (which, broadly speaking, includes northern Iraq and Iran and eastern Turkey) with pride and skill. From *dolmas* to *biryani* to garbanzo bean *shilla,* the food puts an emphasis on bright, tart, fresh flavors—a vegetarian can eat happily here, and a carnivore will appreciate the delicacy with which meat is handled. The *biryani* (a rice dish with peas, raisins, vegetables, spices, and wheat noodles) is a particular pleasure, a soulful, satisfying, and healthy blend of textures and mild, savory flavors.

The Barbary Fig, 720 Grand Ave., St. Paul, MN 55105; (651) 290-2085; thebarbaryfig.com; Downtown St. Paul, 7th St. & Grand Ave.; Mediterranean; $$. This cozy little joint on St. Paul's chi-chi Grand Avenue combines the ambient affluence with the breezy charm of the Mediterranean, particularly in the summer when its patio is up and running. Dishes tend toward the simple, classic, and fresh, with little to no modern fusion. The couscous with *merguez* sausage, ginger, yams, caramelized onions, and currants brings a full-court press of North African flavor that will please most palates. A cup of Turkish coffee is the perfect punctuation to a Barbary Fig meal.

Bars Bakery, 612 Selby Ave., St. Paul, MN 55102; (651) 224-8300; barsbakery.com; Bakery; $$. This new bakery is making big waves in the local baking scene with some of the most indulgent and elegantly prepared baked goods in the area—the caramel rolls alone are worth the drive from Minneapolis, and the rest of the inventory is similarly decadent and pleasing. The caramel rolls date back to the Swede Hollow Cafe (the previous haunt of Bars's founders) and have an outsize reputation. Handmade croissants are also worth exploring—they're only available Friday through Sunday, so time your visit carefully. While the atmosphere is cramped and relatively spartan, it's a fine place to gobble down a quick and delightful breakfast if you're not up for doing takeout.

The Bikery, 904 4th St. South, Stillwater, MN 55082; (651) 439-3834; thebikeryshop.com; Belgian Bakery; $. The Bikery is the original bike shop/cafe/bakery founded by Belgian baker and cycle enthusiast Olivier Vrambout and his mother, and while they've moved on to the **Bikery Du Nord** (below), their tradition of European baked goods remains. It's a charming cafe and/or light breakfast option if you happen to be in the Stillwater area. Seating is limited in the sunny, casual space, and many locals use it as a neighborhood grab-and-go to start their day.

Bikery du Nord, 41 Judd St., Marine, MN 55047; (651) 433-5801; thebikerydunord.com; Belgian Bakery; $. Some of the most ambitious and memorable baked goods in the Twin Cities area reside in this far-flung but beautiful little town on the St. Croix River at the Bikery du Nord. A spin-off of Stillwater's **Bikery** bike shop and bakery (above), Bikery du Nord is a multifaceted powerhouse, serving as a bike shop, cafe, bakery, and Nordic ski outfitter. Try the flakey, beautifully made croissants (and chocolate croissants) and most especially the pear or other fruit galettes when available. The Bikery du Nord Waffle Van acts as the roaming street food arm of the operation and offers waffles and craft beer to visitors (twitter .com/thewafflevan).

Black Sheep Coffee Cafe, 705 Southview Blvd. South, St. Paul, MN 55075; (651) 554-0155; blacksheepcoffee.com; Cafe; $. Minnesota's Third Wave coffee movement (specialized brewing techniques utilizing micro-source and/or in-house roasted beans) manifests itself at a few select coffee shops—Black Sheep is one of them. The shop roasts its beans on-site, and offers made-from-scratch pastries, a full espresso bar, and light meals. Coffee is prepared by well-trained staff using the high-end industry benchmark Clover machine, but other methods ("Chemex, Cova, Aeropress, Mypressi, Pour-over, French Press, and Siphon brews," as per the cafe's website) are also available. The coffee shop is unconnected to the downtown Minneapolis pizza shop of the same name; its name originates from a customer with an Irish grandmother who told the story of how Irish shepherds would keep one black sheep for every 100 white sheep, as a mark of luxury and culture.

The Blue Door Pub, 1811 Selby Ave., St. Paul, MN 55104; (651) 493-1865; thebdp.com; Burgers; $$. One of the premiere better-burger Jucy Lucy joints in the region (some would argue the best, but Nook fans would get militant at that kind of unilateral declaration), The Blue Door serves up cheese-stuffed hamburgers with creative twists to a crowded house. Founded as a cozy neighborhood place, traffic from miles around has contributed to a sometimes nutso, spill-out-the-door crowded atmosphere that the planned establishment of a second location in Minneapolis may help to alleviate. Fans of local brew will enjoy the taps at BDP—while they don't have a ton of draught beers, those present tend to be good, with Surly and Lift Bridge predominating.

Brasa, 777 Grand Ave., St. Paul MN 51505; (651) 224-1302; or 600 E. Hennepin Ave., Minneapolis, MN 55414; (612) 379-3030; brasa .us; Downtown St. Paul, 7th St. & Grand Ave.; Creole; $$. The disarmingly casual Brasa is one of the most creative dining formats in the Twin Cities, although you wouldn't necessarily guess it from the exterior and interior of its restaurants, which are modern, trendy, and relatively unremarkable. Created and helmed by Beard Award–winning Chef Alex Roberts of the top-flight weekend destination **Restaurant Alma** (p. 39), Brasa is a place created for the other five nights of the week. Its food is scratch cooked from local ingredients, big-batch, healthy, slow-cooked, satisfying family fare with smart Southern and Creole twists. Its meats are sold by sizes—for example, an order of pulled chicken smothered in light cream and pepper gravy would serve 1 to 2, a medium 2 to 3, and a large 3 to 4. There's a real soul food influence on the sides, as well—try the corn bread, creamed spinach with jalapeño, and collard greens to kick your meal into the stratosphere.

Bricks, 407 2nd St. # 2, Hudson, WI 54016; (715) 377-7670; eat bricks.com; Neapolitan Pizza, $$. While not generally recognized as a gastronomic mecca, Hudson, Wisconsin has some high points worth mentioning—the tremendous wine, spirits, and beer selection at Casanova Liquor, the wild game meats of Venison America, and the thin-crusted Italian-style pizza of Bricks. Made in the VPN style (Verace Pizza Napoletana, a pizza makers' code that mandates extremely hot ovens, hand-mixed dough, and fresh, local ingredients) Bricks pizzas are simple, well balanced, and marked by classic combinations—fresh basil and tomato sauce, or ham, mushrooms, artichoke hearts, and kalamata olives, or prosciutto, garlic, and arugula. A DOC upgrade option (recommended) lets diners enjoy a pizza featuring imported mozzarella di bufala, made from whole water buffalo milk.

The Bulldog Lowertown, 237 6th St. East, St. Paul, MN 55101; (651) 221-0750; thebulldogmpls.com; Pub Grub; $. The Bulldog boasts a good beer selection, a lively nightlife, and pub grub that puts at least one or two additional spins on classic hamburger and hot dog bar fare. Lowertown boasts big sandwiches served with chips and a pickle spear; Northeast is known for its burgers and gourmet tater tots (try the *togarishi* flavor); and Uptown has Wisconsin-made cheese curds. Northeast is also one of the few area restaurants to put home-cooking favorite tater tot hotdish on its menu, albeit in tarted-up form with braised beef, bechamel, seared Brussels sprouts, and truffled tot. **Additional locations:** The Bulldog Uptown, 2549 Lyndale Ave. South, Minneapolis, MN

55406; (612) 872-8893; The Bullfrog Cajun, 401 E. Hennepin Ave., Minneapolis, MN 55414; (612) 378-2855.

Cheeky Monkey Deli, 525 Selby Ave., St. Paul, MN 55102; (651) 224-6066; cheekymonkeydeli.com; Deli; $$. This sleekly marketed, British-inspired upstart of a deli/bistro has quickly won over fans with its clever treats including a meat loaf that has received favorable ink from hither and yon and a whole range of tasteful sides including a $1 pot of pickles, and house-made salt-and-pepper chips. Though often busy, the atmosphere is cheerful and convivial, and guests feel comfortable even amid the mild clamor of the place.

D-Spot, 705 Century Ave. North, Suite B, Maplewood, MN 55119; (651) 730-7768; eatatdspot.com; Wings; $. Located out of the way in suburban Maplewood, Minnesota, D-Spot brings a wildly different approach to food that merits a drive: Its menu consists almost solely of gourmet chicken wings served up in dozens upon dozens of different flavors. Chef Darin Koch brings a surprisingly haute cuisine eye to lowbrow food, preparing wings with flavor profiles that include coconut milk and peanut butter (the Muay Thai), maple brown sugar and cinnamon (the chicken and waffles) and honey, chilis, and ginger (the ginger). The wings themselves are nothing to trifle with, either—they're moist and tender on the interior and with pleasantly crispy, substantial exteriors. Be sure to sample the Black Widow (soy glaze, fennel, jerk rub) or ginger wings if available—in a menu full of flashy options, they stand out as well-balanced and (particularly) addictive.

Fasika, 510 N. Snelling Ave., St. Paul, MN 55104; (651) 646-4747; fasika.com; Ethiopian; $$. Big portions of deeply spiced Ethiopian food shared family style with rice or *injera* are the draw to this simple mom-and-pop restaurant that has become known as one of the area's go-to spots for East African cuisine. There are few bells and whistles—the place is quite low key and the ambiance is spartan at best—but the overall experience is satisfying.

Finnish Bistro, 2264 Como Ave., St. Paul, MN 55108; (651) 645-9181; finnishbistro.com; Bakery; $$. This casual eatery with a bakery emphasis is one of the few spots in the Cities where Finnish cuisine makes an appearance (most of the Finns settled farther north, in the Iron Range or around the shores of Lake Superior). A cucumber dill sauce makes multiple appearances on the menu, as does a Finnish stuffed meat pie, and french toast made from Finland's famous pulla cardamom bread. A casual atmosphere and reasonable prices make this a nice spot for breakfast or lunch if you happen to be in the St. Anthony Park neighborhood of St. Paul.

Golden's Deli, 275 E. 4th St., St. Paul, MN 55101; (651) 224-8888; goldensdeli.us; Downtown St. Paul, 7th St. & Grand Ave.; Deli; $. Born as a bagel-sandwich vending street cart, Golden's Deli is both a sit-down deli and a table-stand mainstay of the St. Paul Farmer's Market, where its bagels serve as fuel for shoppers cruising for produce and canned goods. This breakfast and lunch spot is no frills (think bagels, burgers, and sandwiches) but satisfying, and it makes a conscious effort to incorporate local food into its offerings. Golden's puts an emphasis on using fresh vegetables whenever possible, which can make the critical difference between a phoned-in sandwich and a winner.

Grand Ole Creamery, 750 Grand Ave., St. Paul, MN 55105; (651) 293-1655; grandolecreamery.com; Downtown St. Paul, 7th St. & Grand Ave.; Ice Cream; $$. Creamy texture (hey, "cream" is right in the name of the place!), five-mini-scoop flavor samplers, and house-made and often fresh waffle cones make Grand Old Creamery one of the most popular ice cream places in the Cities, and one of the most popular places (period) during the hot, humid summers that often plague the area. The atmosphere is vintage ice cream parlor in a way that will strike visitors as either quaint or profoundly dated and musty, but the service is friendly, and some of the more offbeat flavors (such as the sweet cream or honey-flavored choices) have a rich, delicious integrity to them. The next-door and co-owned thin-crust-style **Grand Pizza** is an added draw for those looking for a quick meal before a deluxe ice cream dessert. **Additional location:** 4737 Cedar Ave. South, Minneapolis, MN 55407; (612) 722-2261.

Groveland Tap, 1834 St. Clair Ave., St. Paul, MN 55105; (651) 699-5058; grovelandtap.com; Burgers; $. The cozy, burger-focused St. Paul wing of the Blue Plate chain of restaurants (which also includes **Longfellow Grill** (p. 89), Edina Grill, and Scusi), Groveland Tap is known for its Cajun Lucy, a spicy twist on the cheese-stuffed hamburger that is the go-to tavern fare for South Minneapolis and beyond. The food at this neighborhood staple is simple (think fried cheese curds, french fries, and burgers) and the atmosphere welcoming and convivial. Specials emphasize meat and comfort—dishes such as stuffed meat pies (known as pasties) and pot roast are amply portioned and familiar.

The Hanger Room, 310 Stillwater Rd., Willernie, MN 55090; (651) 429-1477; thehangerroom.com; American; $$$. A gorgeous dark-wood interior and a bar that sweeps like a 1920s luxury car are just the superficial draws to this tastefully conceived eatery 6 miles from downtown Stillwater (and practically next door to the also visit-worthy **Roman Market,** p. 170). Small plates like light-as-air but flavor-rich gnocchi with sun-dried tomatoes and roasted shallots or bing cherry pork belly amuse the palate, and big dry aged steaks satisfy the stomach. The beer supply is a cause for joy, too—wonderfully big-bodied Belgian imports sit shoulder to shoulder with local craft favorites like Stillwater's own Lift Bridge Brewery and Summit special editions, and the fine blended whiskeys and straight bourbons menu is nothing to sneer at, either.

Happy Gnome, 498 Selby Ave., St. Paul, MN 55102; (651) 287-2018; thehappygnome.com; Gastropub; $$. Nearly 100 different draught beers from all over the state, nation, and world make the Happy Gnome one of the best gathering places for brew fanatics in the Twin Cities. This sprawling but cozy bar also features an upstairs private functions area called the Firehouse Room, which is often booked by local groups doing tastings, beer dinners, and other educational beer-focused events. Happy Gnome is also known for its annual firkin fest, a wildly popular gathering dedicated to the appreciation of (dozens upon dozens) of cask ales. The food is relatively simple and contemporary, featuring pub noshes ranging from fancy cheeses to pizzas to burgers to entrees, which often feature an upscale game-centric twist—think bison striploin or Cornish game hens.

Homi, 864 University Ave. West, St. Paul, MN 55104; (651) 222-0655; homirestaurant.com; Mexican; $. The Mexican restaurant called Homi is the sort of place that gives "hole in the wall" a good name—serving mom-and-pop–created comfort food, Homi offers warm service, humble atmosphere, and soul-satisfying good eats from Hidalgo and Veracruz in Mexico. The menu is (arguably too) huge, but dishes such as enchiladas, empanadas, and soups rise to the top, along with the restaurant's well-regarded *chilaquiles*, a dish made from tortilla chips soaked in a tomatillo or chili sauce and topped with cheese, cilantro, and a meat of your choosing. There's a truly vibrant and authentic Mexican food scene in Minneapolis and St. Paul, and visiting Homi is a good way to put your finger on its pulse.

I Nonni, 981 Sibley Memorial Hwy., Lilydale, MN 55118; (651) 905-1081; inonnirestaurant.com; Italian; $$$. Too often in the United States, "Italian food" means "lowbrow Italian-American food" or just plain "peasant food," consisting of absurdly large portions of starchy pasta and red sauce dispensed from plastic bags and metal cans. I Nonni (literally, "the grandparents") takes the cuisine to a more sophisticated level, presenting thoughtful, seasonally inspired high-end Italian classics in a quiet, civilized atmosphere that should be pleasing to those used to a more traditional concept of fine dining. Many of the menu items are sourced to local or regional farms, but the wine and spirits list is all Italian—the emphasis is put on importing Italy as literally and directly as possible. During the warmer part of the year, I Nonni features patio dining overlooking some very attractive man-made ponds and streams. An attached Italian specialty shop (Buon Giornio) offers a variety of imported olives, olive oils, meats, pasta sauces, and cheeses. Quality and price are both substantial.

Lexington Restaurant, 1096 Grand Ave., St. Paul, MN 55105; (651) 222-5878; thelexongrand.com; Downtown St. Paul, 7th St. & Grand Ave.; American; $$$. Old-fashioned to the point of being charmingly stuffy, the Lexington Restaurant (or the Lex, as it's often affectionately known) is a St. Paul institution, having dispensed the likes of steak and shrimp cocktail for over 75 years. A favored destination for wakes, wedding celebrations, and other milestone events that call for pomp and circumstance, the Lex stands at a crossroads, seeking to update its menu in nonthreatening ways (sliders, a "Sonoma salad," coconut shrimp) while preserving the heart of its culinary legacy (liver and onions, Caesar salad, hand-cut steaks brushed with garlic herb butter and served with a potato). Like **Murray's** (p. 37) in downtown Minneapolis, the Lexington is a fine place to travel back in gastronomic history and thoroughly enjoy the taste of the journey.

The Liffey, 175 7th St. West, St. Paul, MN 55102; (651) 556-1420; theliffey.com; Downtown St. Paul, 7th St. & Grand Ave.; Irish Pub; $$. Dazzling beer and whiskey selections, a rooftop patio with a profoundly pleasant view, plus a dedication to detail in the woodwork that gives it a true pub feel make this a popular spot to lift a pint or three in downtown St. Paul. From the bar's roof you can catch views of the St. Paul skyline, the state capitol, and the city's stunning cathedral. The Liffey's part of the Cara Irish Pubs group, so if you dig it you can do a pub crawl and visit Kieran's (downtown Minneapolis), the Local (Nicollet Mall in Minneapolis), and Cooper (St. Louis Park)—all have a similarly commendable dedication to quality spirits menus and traditional Irish interior design.

Muddy Pig, 162 Dale St. North, St. Paul, MN 55102; (651) 254-1030; Gastropub; $$. The more than 50 carefully curated draught beers available at the Muddy Pig are sufficient to put it at the forefront of the wave of beer bars that have sprung up in the Twin Cities in tandem with its local craft beer brewery boom. This dimly lit, boisterous pub is no slouch when it comes to brown liquor,

either, offering respectable lists of bourbons, Scotches, ryes, and Irish whiskeys, as well. The food is simple and honest, including a number of palatable sandwiches and salads, as well as a small list of more ambitious entree options, and service can be brusque and chaotic, so come with a laid-back attitude and a sense of wonderment vis-a-vis beer.

Muffuletta, 2260 Como Ave., St. Paul, MN 55108; (651) 644-9116; muffuletta.com; New American; $$. Muffuletta's namesake New Orleans-born sandwich includes "Fischer Farms ham, spicy capicolla, pistachio mortadella, and Genoa salami piled high with provolone, and smothered in the traditional olive relish," but you don't have to overdo it to dine here—most of its menu items are elegant and light on their feet. The candlelit dining room is cozy but chic, and it's a hard location to beat for romance and well-balanced new American cuisine. The restaurant also shines on Sunday mornings—its brunch is one of the most decadent, well-produced, and beautifully sourced in the Twin Cities, and the chilled-out, sleekly comfortable atmosphere makes it a perfect place to relax and slowly sip a cup of coffee . . . or two. Or three.

On's Thai Kitchen, 1613 University Ave. West, St. Paul, MN 55104; (651) 644-1444; facebook.com/pages/Ons-Thai-Kitchen /167172009993409; Thai; $$. On's Thai Kitchen is the sort of obscure, not particularly inviting place that you're unlikely to stumble upon by chance, which is why it's fortunate that it has become something of a critic and chow-seeker favorite in the Twin

Cities. This slightly dumpy St. Paul Thai restaurant features some of the brightest flavors and liveliest tastes of any of its kin in the area—the quality of ingredients shines through on the plate. Photo-illustrated menus and attentive service make this off-the-beaten-path Thai gem a fine place to bring even a Thai newbie, and veterans of the cuisine will appreciate the spirit that goes into making each dish.

Palumbo's Pizzeria, 454 S. Snelling Ave., St. Paul, MN 55105; (651) 698-0020; palumbospizzeria.com; Pizza; $$. The pleasant little neighborhood gas-fired pizza joint is short on pretense but long on flavor, serving up earnest pizza made with specially sourced Italian pizza flour, panini, and calzone that utilize classic combinations of ingredients. The dining room is cozy and clean, there's rarely a wait, and there's a little semi-sheltered patio that guests can enjoy when the climate allows it. The Eagan, MN-based Ring Mountain Creamery gelato that's served on-site is well worth the calories—it's rich and creamy, and the flavors taste natural and clean.

Patriots Tavern, 145 New England Place, Stillwater, MN 55082; (651) 342-1472; patriotstav.com; New England Tavern; $$. Get to know the Twin Cities and you learn that gastronomic surprises lurk around many (if not most) corners. Still, Patriots Tavern is a shocker: a New England-inspired tavern and eatery in the suburbs that boats a smoky, pork-kissed clam chowder better than many in Boston, and a dedication to scratch recipes and quality ingredients that reflects Northeast specialties to a degree you wouldn't expect based on the tavern's Potemkin Village-goes-New Hampshire subdevelopment surroundings. The owners (the Pilrain brothers, who have done a similarly inspiring job with Italian-American themed **Roma Restaurant,** below) have done a superb job with the details, down to Boston cream pie, which, while not a by-the-books rendition of the East Coast dessert, is a finely balanced delicious example of the species. The restaurant's crowning glory is a lobster roll (served, as is appropriate, on split, toasted thick-cut bread) that would stand up to a respectable (if somewhat overdressed with mayo) specimen from Maine itself. See Chef Brent Pilrain's recipe for **Dingle Fish Pie** on page 257.

Roman Market and Roma Restaurant, 460 Stillwater Rd., Willernie, MN 55090; (651) 653-4733; roman-market.com; Italian-American; $$. There may be no cuisine more comforting than Italian-American, and there may be no cuisine more often maligned by low-quality ingredients and lazy presentation. Roma Restaurant turns this unpleasant trend on its head—between the meat prepared by its in-house butcher shop and fresh-tasting, often locally sourced ingredients, the place manages to rehabilitate the entire genre. The sublimely balanced fig, prosciutto, and balsamic vinegar pizza was good enough to impress a jaded visiting New Jerseyite—which says a lot—the local draft beer selection is small but well curated, and the pasta dishes manage to be both primally satisfying and unpretentiously thoughtful. Start out with the *spirito* (a flatbread with three elegantly simple spreads) if you want to kick your meal off right. The restaurant's owners (Brent and Brian Pilrain) did well enough with Roma that they opened a second place, the equally impressive and soulful **Patriots Tavern** (p. 169). See Chef Brent Pilrain's recipe for **Balsamico Pizza** on page 259.

Ruam Mit Thai Cafe, 475 Saint Peter St., St. Paul, MN 55102; ruam-mit-thai.net; Downtown St. Paul, 7th St. & Grand Ave.; Thai; $$. This earnest little Thai restaurant feels like a discount diner but serves up food with a depth of spice and funky flavor that surpasses most of the fancified Uptown Thai joints by a long shot. The traditional Thai food flavor pillars of sweet, sour, acidic, and earthy are present in most if not all of the dishes served, and when you get a dish with a peanut component, that taste is funky and almost smoky, not merely sweet like Skippy or Jif.

Salut Bar Americain, 5034 France Ave. South, Edina, MN 55424; (952) 929-3764; salutbaramericain.com; Downtown St. Paul, 7th St. & Grand Ave.; French; $$$. With its French bistro fare skillfully interpreted for Middle American palates, the trendy and somewhat spendy Salut skillfully harnesses and satisfies the desires of well-heeled retail therapy participants hitting either the Edina or Grand

Avenue shopping districts, delivering unto them a variety of steak frites, entrees like duck a l'orange or rabbit gnocchi or a decent cassoulet (look to **Meritage,** p. 151, in St. Paul for the real deal on that front, however). Mirrors and vintage-y Continental touches make for a cohesive and relevant atmosphere, and the *pommes frites* are quite good, named "Best Fries in the Twin Cities" at one point by *Mpls.St. Paul Magazine.* The general clamor and professional service ethic mean that you can crash the joint with a big shopping-bag-laden group or a squad of little ones, and the house will handle it with aplomb. **Additional location:** 917 Grand Ave., St. Paul, MN 55105; (651) 917-2345.

Senor Wong, 111 Kellogg Blvd. East, St. Paul, MN 55101; (651) 224-2019; senorwong.com; Downtown St. Paul, 7th St. & Grand Ave.; Fusion; $$. Taking a pretty strong cue from the Uptown-based multicultural pound-a-cocktail drinking zone known as Chino Latino, Senor Wong specializes in small, clever plates of food that start with the cuisines of Asia and Latin America and take flight from there. Tacos, fried rice, stir-fries, and pho anchor the menu, and there are many amusing bites from lettuce wraps to short ribs to fill the spaces in between. Like Chino, the shiny, dimly lit, musically jumpin' Senor Wong has a nightclub-meets-bistro thing going on, and its hours are unusually late for St. Paul, doing business until 2 in the morning on Thursday through Saturday nights. Amusements including bingo, trivia, live DJs, and karaoke spice up the restaurant's midweek atmosphere. The restaurant has recently added a craft beer component, featuring brewery dinners and kegs of sometimes hard-to-find specialty beers from the likes of Surly and Goose Island.

Smalley's Caribbean Barbeque and Pirate Bar, 423 Main St., Stillwater, MN 55082; (651) 439-5375; smalleyspiratebbq.com; Caribbean; $$. Two patios, rum drinks, and festive pirate- and/or Caribbean-themed decor (a lovely Red Stripe mural, skeletons with hooks on their hands, and so forth) are the main draws to this centrally located novelty establishment, which features unevenly pre-pared barbecue and often chronically over-sweet sides. Stick to the beer and straightforward fare like ham-burgers, and your visit can be a pleasant one.

Snuffy's Malt Shop, 4502 Valley View Rd., Edina, MN 55424; (952) 920-0949; snuffysmaltshop.com; Diner; $$. Thick, creamy malts and back-to-basics crispy burgers are the cornerstones of this local chain, each location of which feels like a singularly neighborhood place despite there being five of them scattered throughout the area. It may be the comfy booths, or the sim-plicity of the menu, or the pleasure in enjoying something as uncomplicated as a malt shop in the era of video chats and social media. **Additional locations:** 244 Cleveland Ave. South, St. Paul, MN 55105; (651) 690-1846; 17519 Minnetonka Blvd., Minnetonka, MN 55345; (952) 475-1850; 1125 Larpenteur Ave. West, St. Paul, MN 55113; (651) 488-0241.

Sole Cafe, 684 N. Snelling Ave., St. Paul, MN 55104; (651) 644-2068; solecafe.weebly.com; Korean; $$. I don't have a Korean grandmother, but if I did, I imagine that her cooking would taste very much like what's on offer in the humble, hole-in-the-wall St. Paul eatery known as Sole Cafe. Flavors are vibrant and bright, the *banchan* (assorted, mostly pickled sides including kimchi) are plentiful and generous, and the MSG-free food has that unquantifiable funky, deep, properly seasoned charm that is the number one reason to pop 'round to little mom-and-pop ethnic shops like this one. Try the *haemul pajeon* (seafood-and-chives pancake) if you're in the mood for something a bit more exciting than *bibimbap* (a mixed crispy rice and vegetable dish served with a fried egg)—you won't regret it.

Sweets Bakeshop, 2042 Marshall Ave., St. Paul, MN 55104; sweetsbakeshop.com; Bakery; $$. When James Beard-award-winning local critic and author Dara Moskowitz Grumdahl favorably compared the macarons from Sweets to those she regularly enjoys in Paris, local bakery fans sat up and took notice. The stuff at Sweets is no joke—while the flavors of their macarons and cupcakes are reasonably simple and straightforward (a salted caramel cupcake, mint basil or lavender macarons), the execution and presentation are meticulous, and the flavors pure, simple, thrilling but not over-sweet, and more or less swoon-inducing. The shop also makes whimsical and skillfully executed custom cakes that are show-stoppers for parties, weddings, and other gatherings where there's pressure to impress. **Additional location:** 4747 Nicollet Ave. South, Minneapolis, MN 55419; (612) 208-0672.

Tanpopo Restaurant, 308 Prince St. #140, St. Paul, MN 55101; (651) 209-6527; tanpoporestaurant.com; Downtown St. Paul, 7th St. & Grand Ave.; Japanese; $$$. One of the key traits of the Japanese aesthetic—perhaps, arguably, the key defining trait—is minimalism. That's a quality that the impeccably elegant Tanpopo has in spades. Its dining room is spare but tastefully defined by hardwood floors and wooden trim, and its menu is short and simple, focused on soba and udon noodle dishes and a few other tastes. Set meals and fish specials pop up, but this is no urban bar-crawl sushi joint. It's a place to quietly sip and appreciate cuisine made with poise and balance, and is a perfect place to catch up with a friend or enjoy an intimate evening with a favorite companion. The steamy warmth of the noodles served here is a great antidote to winter, and a visit to Tanpopo on a subzero evening can be a profoundly restorative experience. At least until you have to walk back out to your car.

W.A. Frost & Co., 374 Selby Ave., St. Paul, MN 55102; (651) 224-5715; wafrost.com; New American; $$$. The historic Dacotah Building space occupied by W.A. Frost and Company since 1975 is gorgeous, inside and out. Inside: It's laid out with oriental rugs, exposed brick and beam construction, and period wallpaper. Outside, in warm weather: a courtyard-style garden patio with comfortable but classy rattan furniture and greenery at all levels. The 3,000-bottle wine cellar will leave few palates unsatisfied, and the food is luxe with a locavore touch—dishes like Wild Acres pheasant breast and pan-roasted steelhead trout with Thielen Family bacon call out their purveyors in their titles, and other entrees like cocoa-crusted elk striploin embrace the wild game heritage that makes Midwestern cabin cooking the sometimes majestic enterprise that it is. The restaurant also operates two private dining rooms that are a good match for large, higher-end functions.

Regional Gastronomic Info

Purveyors &
Specialties

If you learn about and meet a region's purveyors, you're more than halfway to understanding its food. The bakers, brewers, farmers, foragers, vintners, distillers, and others who help set the tables of Minneapolis and St. Paul also set the tone for Upper Midwestern cuisine—their products are the starting point for local menus and the heart of why local food tastes, well, "local." The area's shops and markets are full of local wares (even in winter!), and if you're in town with a bit of time on your hands, keep your eyes peeled for fine food made right here in Minnesota and Wisconsin.

Annona Gourmet, 2907 Pentagon Dr., Minneapolis, MN 55418; (612) 354-2927; annonagourmet.com. Annona Gourmet was the tip of an olive oil and vinegar iceberg that has fully manifested itself in the Twin Cities—along with four or five other stores that could be its mirror image (including Vinaigrette in Linden Hills and the Stillwater Olive Oil Company in Stillwater), Annona Gourmet's stock in trade is big, beautiful carboys from which come a flow of high-end balsamic vinegars and specialty olive oils. Flavored or pure, grassy or sweet, imported or domestic—it's all here, and, best of all, it's all easy to sample with the in-house system of plain bread and miniature paper sample cups that allow you to taste before you commit. The whole experience is eminently civilized, and if you're in town for long enough to do some baking and cooking, it can take your chef game up to the next level. Pro tip: Mango balsamic vinegar tastes mind-blowing when drizzled on vanilla ice cream.

Bill's Imported Foods, 721 W. Lake St., Minneapolis, MN 55408; (612) 827-2892; billsimportedfoods.com. At the bustling Lyndale and Lake intersection of Uptown is this local staple known for its oils, imported canned goods, and its amazingly broad array of fetas that may be the most comprehensive in the state. In contrast to **Holy Land** (below), Bill's offers a broader spread of Mediterranean imports, and their staff tends to be both friendly and knowledge-able about their sometimes esoteric products. A key place to stop if you're hunting for phyllo dough, olive oil, dried fruit, fresh pita, or olives of all varieties.

France 44 Wine & Spirits, 4351 France Ave. South, Minneapolis, MN 55410; (612) 925-3252; france44.com. Along with **Surdyk's** (see p. 183), France 44 is one of the heavy hitters on the Twin Cities fine foods scene. At both of France 44's locations, gourmet cheese is sold by the pound or incorporated into luxe sandwiches. The flagship store (at France Avenue and 44th Street) offers a head-spinning collection of wine, liquor, and craft beer for sale, including some difficult-to-find imports. Many of the bottles are marked for sampling, and the "try-before-you-buy" policy on spirits can save the customer many a $50 (or $100) accident. The staff is universally well informed, an obvious asset to the customer.

Golden Fig, 790 Grand Ave., St. Paul, MN 55105; (651) 602-0144; goldenfig.com. St. Paul's Golden Fig is one of the area's prime go-tos for Upper Midwestern specialty foods—from cheese to spice blends to heritage chicken to jams and bread mixes, this crowded little nook of a store is a prime gathering place for local authors and locavore cooks. Like **Local D'Lish** (see p. 183), it's half store, half scene, all Midwestern. Golden Fig is also part of the bigger Grand Avenue food and restaurant scene, which lends itself to be a destination on an afternoon-long stroll of the street.

Holy Land Bakery, 920 E. Lake St., Minneapolis, MN 55407; (612) 870-6104; holylandbrand.com. Holy Land is more than a store—this local chain serves up falafel and gyros, makes and sells its own Middle Eastern foods and sauces, acts as a bakery and prime place to purchase decent olive oil for good prices, and is a clearinghouse of information for new immigrants to the United States from Middle Eastern countries. In short: it's a community pillar, and a first stop for locals hoping to cook (or just purchase and enjoy) Middle Eastern food. Holy Land also brings its goods to the Minnesota State Fair, putting a pleasant spin on the typical "what have you fried and put on a stick" idea that is the norm.

Ingebretsen's, 1601 E. Lake St., Minneapolis, MN 55407; (612) 729-9333 or (800) 279-9333; ingebretsens.com. A Mecca for all things Scandinavian and food-related, the deli known as Ingebretsen's has been a going concern under one name or another in various locations since 1921. It's the East Lake Street location that stuck, at a time when the neighborhood (and residential areas clear up to Cedar Riverside) was still thick with Swedes and Norwegians. In the years since, the East Lake neighborhood has taken on a distinctly Latino and East African flavor, but Ingebretsen's persists, serving up ethnic favorites like *lefse*, *lutefisk*, Swedish meatball mix, sausages, Scandinavian cheeses, rye breads, and more. An attached gift shop features a variety of Scandinavian ornaments, decorative items, servingware, greeting cards, and more, making Ingebretsen's a one-stop shop for your northern European food and gift needs. As a cultural preserve, it's a civic treasure, and if you're game for experimenting with rye bread, fish paste, and traditional sausages and luncheon meats, it's a heck of a good stop for those on a mission to make *smorrebrod* (open-faced sandwiches).

Lake Elmo Wine Company, 3511 Lake Elmo Ave. North, Lake Elmo, MN 55042; (651) 621-1520; lakeelmowine.com. Established by Kim Ommerborn, a New York-based importer who spent her formative years in the business traveling the world and becoming educated about wine, the Lake Elmo Wine Company is a pleasant surprise in the Cities' eastern suburbs: a small independent wine shop with a carefully curated selection and a knowledgeable owner on-site to guide customers through the process of selecting the right wine. While it's dwarfed by the area's wine and liquor giants (**Surdyk's,** see below, and **France 44,** see p. 180, for example), the Lake Elmo Wine Company offers boutique service and a pleasantly modestly priced inventory. Male customers will appreciate the shop's Beer Cave, a temperature-controlled chamber stocked with artisanal brews.

Lake Street Wine and Spirits, 404 W. Lake St., Minneapolis, MN 55408; (612) 354-7194; lakewinespirits.com. A newly established specialty store in the tradition of **France 44** (see p. 180) and **Surdyk's** (see below), Lake Street is a one-stop shop for those hoping to serve swanky cocktails and/or sophisticated wine and/or a cheese plate to die for. Noted cheese merchant Ken Liss lends his services to the cheese shop, which features an exceptional collection of imported Spanish cheeses, crackers, and meats, including the pricey and coveted *jamon serrano*.

Local D'Lish, 208 N. 1st St., Minneapolis, MN 55401; (612) 886-3047; localdlish.com. Newly established Local D'Lish brings a farmers' market–type aesthetic to a specialty store, concentrating on the fruits (literally and figuratively) of local purveyors. Offering classes, demos, CSA drop-offs, and an indoor winter farmers' market on the third Saturday of each month from November through April, Local D'Lish represents one of the most ambitious efforts yet to bring the Midwestern farm into the Minneapolis urban environment.

Surdyk's, 303 E. Hennepin Ave., Minneapolis, MN 55414; (612) 379-3232; surdyks.com. For the Scotch, tequila, or rum nut, Surdyk's in Northeast Minneapolis looks like heaven fallen to Earth. An extensive wine and sake selection augments the spirits section, and an attached cheese shop sells a fine selection of local and international cheeses. The store has also taken on a reputation as a lunch destination—its gourmet sandwiches and baked goods are as good as any in the city, restaurants included.

United Noodles, 2015 E. 24th St., Minneapolis, MN 55404; (612) 721-6677; unitednoodles.com. United Noodles is a triple threat (at least)—it's an Asian produce market, featuring everything from the familiar to durian. It's a Japanese specialty market, with the specialized sauces, toppings, mixes, noodles, and other staples needed to pull off authentic or semi-authentic re-creations of Japanese favorites. And it's a pan-Asian supermarket with tastes from Korea, China, Vietnam, and beyond. Actually, make it a quadruple threat—the humble on-site restaurant offers affordable but reinvigorating Asian barbecue- and soup-based dishes for a song. Not much for atmosphere, but long on flavor and gritty charm.

Locally Made Regional Specialties

Beyond beer and meat, a whole host of Minnesota-made food products bring a sheen of local pride to the Twin Cities food scene.

Alemar Cheese Company, 622 N. Riverfront Dr., Mankato, MN 56001; (507) 385-1004; alemarcheese.com. Alemar makes a Camembert-style cheese called Bent River that is locally beloved and haunts a large percentage of cheese plates served up by upscale restaurants in the Twin Cities area. It took third place in the Camembert group during judging at the American Cheese Society contest in 2011, besting dozens of others with its clean, creamy flavor.

Cedar Summit Butter, (952) 758-6886; cedarsummit.com. Cedar Summit is a small but growing creamery in New Prague, Minnesota, that uses local cows' milk to make high-fat, small-batch, never-frozen butter that stands up to European imports in terms of its applications in baking and other high-profile dishes that bring dairy to the forefront. If you haven't tried local artisanal butter before, it's worth seeking out at an area specialty store, and if you have, you appreciate what makes a good local butter so valuable to a dining scene.

Clem's Homegrown Popcorn of Castle Rock. Clem's popcorn is hand-picked, hand-sorted, and called by at least one reputable regional food authority (author Brett Laidlaw) "the best popcorn in the world." Composed of big, fluffy kernels that rarely if ever fail to pop, Clem's is of gourmet quality, and can be ordered directly from the growers if you fail to find it in local stores (it's sold at specialty shops and country markets). Contact Cindy Plash to order (cplash@frontiernet.net; 651-460-8034).

Deena's Gourmet, (651) 329-3045; deenasgourmet.com. Deena's is a bit of an odd duck as local food companies go—it's not making *lutefisk* or *lefse,* but rather hummus—and very well-regarded hummus, at that. A roasted red pepper and feta variety is a local favorite, but the more conventional varieties are also popular and widely available at local co-ops and specialty stores.

Faribault Dairy, (507) 334-5260; faribaultdairy.com. The sandstone cheese caves of Faribault, Minnesota, have the distinction of being the largest such caves in the country. Faribault Dairy uses them to age and store a great quantity of artisan cheese, including a blue and a gorgonzola that they are regionally famous for, and an upscale brand of cave-finished cheddar known as Fini. Cave aging, done properly, can help impart a mellow depth of flavor that can turn passable cheese into excellent cheese, and Faribault uses its greatest asset with skill, making one of the best cheeses in the state and a cheese that is certainly competitive with the world-class product being made in neighboring Wisconsin.

Izzy's Ice Cream Cafe, 2034 Marshall Ave., St. Paul, MN 55104; (651) 603-1458; izzysicecream.com. Izzy's ice cream is famous for two things: the "izzy scoop," a small bonus scoop of ice cream that comes with every cone sold on-site at its St. Paul ice cream shop, and its long lines. Late into the night on summer evenings, residents will queue up for a taste of the rich, creamy, creatively flavored stuff that Izzy's puts out by the gallon. The wait may go down in the near future—the company (as of this writing) is planning a major expansion and a full-fledged factory in the near future.

Lucille's Kitchen Garden, lucilleskitchengarden.com. Lucille's makes nationally recognized jam in flavors that would likely be incomprehensible to the grandmotherly jam-makers of days of yore—favorites include Minnesota Mead Jelly, Garlic Pepper Jam, and Cranberry White Balsamic Chutney. A sophisticated sense of

LUTEFISK

If you're even passingly familiar with Minnesota food folkways, you're probably familiar with the infamous but locally crucial Christmas-time dish of *lutefisk* (lye-cured codfish). Prepared incorrectly, it can have a texture that is most generously described as "off-putting," but old-school Norwegians swear by it, at least publicly. The **Olsen Fish Company** (2115 N. 2nd St., Minneapolis, MN 55411; 612-287-0838; olsenfish.com) makes the best-known local product, and specialty stores like **Ingebretsen's** in South Minneapolis (1601 E. Lake St., Minneapolis, MN 55407; 612-729-9333 or 800-279-9333; ingebretsens.com) vend it to the general public, no apologies offered.

balance and an interplay between sweet and savory typifies Lucille's products, as does a willingness to play with atypical ingredients including wine and savory herbs. Lucille's jams excel at savory culinary applications—applied to fish or pork, for example, they can provide a unique and profound finishing flavor to an otherwise under-flavored dish.

1919 Classic American Draft Root Beer, (888) NO.1.Soda; 1919rootbeer.com. There are a number of local root beers (Killebrew and Dorothy's Isle of Pines being among the two most prominent,

FINDING THE BEST SMOKED FISH

Minnesota's North Shore is nationally known for its hand-smoked fish—Lake Superior fish such as whitefish and herring join imports (typically salmon) destined for the smokehouse, where a careful application of heat and burned wood turns fresh raw fish into a golden-lacquered, durable trade good that is equally delicious on a saltine, with a bagel and cream cheese, or just straight up on its own. **Northern Waters Smokehaus** (DeWitt-Seitz Marketplace, 394 Lake Ave. South, Suite 106, Duluth, MN 55802; 218-724-7307 or 888-663-7800; northernwaterssmokehaus.com) or **Russ Kendall's Smokehouse** (149 Scenic Dr., Knife River, MN 55609; 218-834-5995) are two of the most prominent places to frequent, the former preferred by some modern gourmets, the latter by many traditionalists. Both, it should be noted, put out an excellent product.

with rich back stories and hard-core devotees), but 1919 has developed an outsize reputation as a root beer for grown-ups. Its clean taste profile (provided in part by the use of natural sugar rather than corn syrup) and balance between sweetness and spice make it a favorite for root beer fanatics with strong opinions, and is sufficiently well regarded that it sometimes makes its way into alcoholic cocktails. It's brewed on-site at the historic New Ulm brewery of Schell's, a company also responsible for making the locally legendary Grain Belt Premium, a working-class mainstay of taverns from Northeast Minneapolis to the eastern reaches of St. Paul.

Nordic Ware, (877) 466-7342; nordicware .com. If you've ever had a Bundt cake, you have local manufacturer Nordic Ware to thank—the company's factory store (4925 Hwy. 7, Minneapolis, MN 55416; 952-924-9672; nordicware.com/about/factory-store) offers a dizzying variety of pots, pans, utensils, specialty Scandinavian cooking implements, and more beyond the dozens (or was it hundreds?) of Bundt pans on its shelves.

Phillips Distilling of Minneapolis, (612) 362-7500; phillips distilling.com. Phillips provides at least two mainstay tipples for the local scene: Its Prairie Organic vodka is one of the liquors of choice for the area's better barkeeps, and the company makes a classic and nicely balanced peppermint schnapps that ends up in a good percentage of the thermoses of hot cocoa brought along on ice fishing expeditions.

The Sand Creek Brewing Co., 320 Pierce St., Black River Falls, WI 54615; (715) 284-7553; sandcreekbrewing.com. Every hard lemonade that I've ever tasted has been a hellish, chemical-laden sugar bomb—with the exception of the stuff made by the brewers at Sand Creek in Black River Falls, Wisconsin. If you spot their product, snatch it up—it's a clean, pleasingly citric flavor with none of the pitfalls that typically bedevil its peers. It's a revelation that at least partially redeems its previously hopeless category of drinks.

Smude's Sunflower Oil. Smude's Sunflower Oil represents what could be the tiny tip of a large iceberg—Midwestern farmers and consumers searching for local alternatives to olive oil. Locavore restaurants (including **Spoonriver**, p. 42; **Birchwood Cafe**, p. 17; **Common Roots**, p. 67; **Grand Cafe**, p. 80; and **Heartland**, p. 148) use Smude's oil in order to cook high-end food with a thoroughly local flourish. The flavor of the oil is light, buttery, and relatively neutral, making it a fine base for both frying and applications such as vinaigrettes.

Spring Grove Soda Pop, Inc., 215 2nd Ave. Northwest, Spring Grove, MN 55974; (507) 498-3424; springgrovesoda.com. Nostalgia-inducing Spring Grove soda is one of a few local companies that makes a quality product—its pure cane sugar base helps give its sodas a refreshing taste, and its flavors are both sophisticated and traditional, including a brilliantly reinvigorating lemon sour flavor and a strawberry flavor that pays homage to sodas from the days of yore. The pop shows up sporadically at local stores, but is generally available at Midtown Global Market's Produce Exchange.

Star Prairie Trout Farm, 400 Hill Ave., Star Prairie, WI 54026; (715) 248-3633; starprairietrout.com. The cold, spring-fed streams and pools of Star Prairie Trout make for fish that grow more slowly than trout raised in warmer waters—but the happy side of the trade-off is that Star Prairie trout have firmer flesh and a cleaner taste. It's difficult to find a high-end restaurant in the Twin Cities that doesn't at least occasionally offer Star Prairie trout as a

SPAM in Minnesota?

While it may not strike you as "local" to anywhere, SPAM is actually a Minnesota product, made by the Hormel Corporation of Austin, Minnesota. Per Wikipedia, SPAM (the name derived from "spiced ham") is made from "chopped pork shoulder meat, with ham meat added, salt, water, modified potato starch as a binder, and sodium nitrite as a preservative." If that's the sort of thing you like, welcome to SPAM's birthplace. Of course, if you want to see SPAM deeply integrated into the culinary arts, Hawaii is where you need to go—per capita, Hawaiians eat more SPAM than residents of any other state.

special, and many restaurants make these Wisconsin-raised fish into a mainstay of their seafood menus. And if the weather's warm and you're craving some easy trout-fishing action with on-site cleaning, Star Prairie is open to amateur anglers. Just be warned—catching a fish amid the tens of thousands on-site is as easy as shooting fish in a barrel.

The Twin Cities Bakery Boom

The general boom of high-end and place-specific food in the Twin Cities perhaps buoyed bakeries faster than it has lifted any other specialty (possible and complementary exception: coffee). Far from being dominated by dour, Midwestern whitebread; soft, spongy baguettes; insultingly bad bagels; and oversweetened, mediocre baked desserts, the one-time flour milling champion of the world "Mill City" of Minneapolis and its sibling St. Paul have seen a tidal wave of more thoughtful offerings. They include delicate French macarons that have been compared to their kin in France by knowledgeable tasters, gourmet doughnuts that could hold their own in Portland or San Francisco, rich, luscious bars and cakes that are indulgent but well-balanced, and breads with real flavor, real crumb, and real crust.

The big trends are bread with more flavor, crust, and substance, and sweets that are both more balanced (not just sugar overkill) and more subtly flavored with local and/or natural ingredients. High-end cupcakes came (and, to some extent, went) with the national craze—high-end French macarons seem to have more traction.

Rustica (p. 119) and its brilliant baguettes and killer cookies is one of the pioneers, but a new wave of high-end baked goods have radically transformed the scene since as recently as 2008 or 2009.

Owner John Kraus of **Patisserie 46** (p. 106) has a European baking pedigree and spent a dozen years teaching at the French Pastry School in Chicago before opening his shop in the Kingfield neighborhood of Minneapolis. It ascended to the top of local "best of" lists like a bullet, thanks to its delicate, well-balanced, beautifully crafted teacakes, croissants, cookies, eclairs, and other baked specialties rarely seen outside of Europe. The macarons are vivid and have perfect crispy-chewy texture, and the overall vibe is of effortless sophistication. Taking a cup of coffee with a tiny, flavorful cake on the side at Patisserie 46 may be one of the most civilized moments you can have in a city that's already quite civilized. And if you want to make a splash at a dinner party, bring along one of the bakery's massive boule loaves—it'll feed a dozen people and generate oohs and aahs as it's presented.

When Anne Rucker, a lawyer turned baker, founded **Bogart Loves** (facebook.com/bogartloves; bogartloves.blogspot.com), she didn't anticipate the reaction her treats would generate from the crowds at the Kingfield farmers' market; she's had to scale up quickly and has seen her business evolve from a sideline hobby to a local brand. Her indulgent but upscale goodies include Nutella-filled brioches, maple-bacon doughnuts, whoopie pies, and salted caramel brownies. Rucker is typical of many of the new food entre-preneurs in the area, who are moving from white-collar professions into food carts and farmers' market stalls, reinventing themselves from talkers and writers into makers and doers.

Solveig Tofte's first name means "Sun Street," and that's also the name of her new bakery, **Sun Street Breads** (p. 128), fast becoming a South Minneapolis staple. From breads like figgy rye and Harriet Beer bread (made with the brewery's popular West Side IPA) to breakfasts like biscuits and gravy and sweets like turnovers and cinnamon "downtowners," the fresh little bakery covers a lot of ground and has become a popular breakfast destination for its neighborhood.

Sweets Bakeshop (p. 174) makes macarons that local food author and critic Dara Moskowitz Grumdahl said "rival Ladurée's in Paris," and that—honestly—should be enough of an endorsement to get you through the doors. But if it isn't, consider that this new two-shop mini-empire of macarons and tiny cupcakes also makes some of the best sculpted character cakes in the Cities, and features flavors such as sweet corn and mojito. Seasonal menu shifts add yet more interest—last autumn saw Vampire's Desire (chocolate ganache and raspberry) in October, for example. The St. Paul location is also next to an **Izzy's Ice Cream** shop (p. 149), just in case the sugar from the cupcakes and macarons isn't sufficient to get you through the afternoon.

If there's a bakery worth driving 30 minutes to get to, it may be **YoYo Donuts & Coffee Bar** (5757 Sanibel Dr., Minnetonka, MN 55343; 952-960-1800; yoyodonuts.com), which is fortunate—they're located out in the suburb of Minnetonka, but they're doing some of the best breakfast pastries in the whole region. The maple-bacon long john is a thing of real beauty, expertly balancing the natural sweetness of the glaze with the salty, pork-inflected crunch of the bacon. This thing is no novelty—it's a legitimately delicious way to start the day, especially when accompanied by a cup of coffee. The doughnuts are also made without preservatives or dough extenders, so they boast a freshness that supermarket and national doughnut chains would envy. While you're out at YoYo, stop over at the nearby **Pairings Food and Wine Market** (6001 Shady Oak Rd., Minnetonka, MN 55343; 952-426-0522; pairingsfoodandwine.com), which has a killer beer selection and a number of thoughtfully prepared casual dining options.

The best thing at **Bars Bakery** (612 Selby Ave., St. Paul, MN 55102; 651-224-8300; barsbakery.com) in St. Paul is not a bar at all—it's a caramel roll that gained local fame at a previous establishment, the Swede Hollow Cafe. Requisitely sweet and tender, the caramel on this roll is freshly made and has a beautiful depth of flavor that transforms this treat from decent to absolutely extraordinary. The bars (brownies, lemon bars, and so forth) are made with love and care, and while the overall vibe is Midwest, the baking chops are internationally respectable.

Chef Michelle Gayer of the **Salty Tart** (920 E. Lake St., Minneapolis, MN 55407; 612-874-9206; saltytart.com) has great credentials: hailing from Charlie Trotter's Restaurant and having spent time at the internationally famous La Brea Bakery and the locally famous **La Belle Vie** (p. 29), she started on strong footing and has gotten stronger from there, garnering a series of James Beard award nominations for her work at the Midtown Global Market in South Minneapolis. Seasonal and local ingredients drive Salty Tart's menu, and it's not unusual to see local brewers or cheesemakers represented in the bakery case. Her Surly beer–infused chocolate chocolate cupcake with crunchy chocolate topping is a vital must-try if it crosses your path.

Meat the Locals: The Hot Dago & the Jucy Lucy

As Philly has its cheesesteak, New York has its pizza, and Chicago has its hot dog, so do the Twin Cities have their own particular native street food favorites. Street food is meant to be cheap, portable, and substantial, and the **Jucy Lucy** of Minneapolis is three for three. (Well, perhaps two for three when its cheese starts leaking, but we'll get to that in a moment.)

The Jucy Lucy is a cheese-stuffed hamburger that became popular in the 3.2 bars (said as "three two bars") of South Minneapolis, where liquor laws prohibited the serving of beer with an alcohol content stronger than 3.2 percent. Its original heyday was the 1950s and '60s, but the Jucy has persisted to the modern era and seen itself reinvented in a number of guises and locations that would likely make its original popularizers' heads spin.

Conventional wisdom suggests that there are two main contenders for the "original Jucy Lucy" throne, both located in South Minneapolis: **Matt's Bar** (p. 34) and the **5-8 Club Tavern & Grill** (p. 23). If you drill down on the facts, Matt's Bar has the edge, and it triumphs when it comes to atmosphere, too—it's a homey, dark, intimate, charming hole-in-the-wall place, haunted by generations of locals but enough of a tourist destination that the cash till hums with dollars from distant cities. The burger itself isn't much to speak of, unfortunately—flavorless cheese and low-grade meat make it a yawn from a flavor perspective, and the fries are thoroughly without character. Still, it's a splash of local color and a hell of a lot of fun to visit. The same can't quite be said for the 5-8 Club, which has an antiseptic, TGI Friday's feel to its interior and underseasoned burgers that, it must be said, have an overall quality advantage over Matt's. As a footnote: A third South Minneapolis bar, **Adrian's** (48th and Chicago Ave. South, Minneapolis, MN 55417; 612-824-4011; adrianstavern.com), may be the actual origin point of the burger, but it's far more modest about bragging up its Jucy, no doubt to its commercial disadvantage.

Strangely enough, the best Jucy Lucys now get made in St. Paul. **The Nook** (see p. 152), an unassuming sports bar near Cretin-Derham Hall, uses superior-grade cheese and fresh bakery buns to make a far tastier Jucy Lucy than its cross-town rivals. And the relatively newly founded **The Blue Door Pub** (p. 158)—based in St. Paul, but opening a new location in Minneapolis neighborhood of Longfellow—dresses up its Lucys with a variety of high-concept themes, including a spicy, peanut-butter-kissed Thai variation and a Breakfast Blucy featuring thick-cut bacon and a fried egg.

As the Jucy Lucy is to Minneapolis, the **hot dago** is to St. Paul. If you're reading this and thinking, "hold the phone, isn't 'dago' a rather offensive term once applied pejoratively to Italian Americans?" you should know that you're absolutely right, and that absolutely nobody native to the Twin Cities in general and St. Paul in particular thinks of ethnic hostility when they hear the word "dago" used in a gastronomic context. (I wrote about the evolving etymology of the word "dago" in my book *Minnesota Lunch: From Pasties to Banh Mi*.)

In this part of the country a dago is a sandwich built around a spicy Italian sausage patty. From there, the ingredients vary a little bit, but melted cheese, marinara, and spicy peppers tend to be part of the story. Ciabatta bread generally makes the sandwich into a messy but hand-holdable meal, unless it's served as a gooey open-faced mess as it is at **DeGidio's** (p. 146) or as a neat, burger-like package as it is at **Dusty's** in Northeast Minneapolis (p. 22).

And as the Jucy has gone upscale at **The Blue Door** (p. 158) and **The Nook** (p. 152), so has the dago stepped squarely into the 21st century at **Roma** (p. 170), where it sports a lovely, kicky, house-made *giardiniera* relish and an expertly made house-ground sausage patty.

A Street Food Revolution

In 2008, *City Pages* food critic Rachel Hutton described the local street food scene in bleak terms: "Here in Minneapolis, street food amounts to three Nicollet Mall hot dog vendors and a few renegade merchants with portable coolers of queso-coated corncobs or mango with chili powder. Frankly, if you're looking for variety, you'd be better off Dumpster diving."

What a difference a few years makes.

Major changes to city ordinances in both Minneapolis and St. Paul in 2010 liberalized restrictions on where street trucks and carts can operate, and led to a street food explosion that has put Minneapolis-St. Paul on track with any city in the country, save perhaps for Los Angeles or New York.

Even before the law changes, the pioneering **Chef Shack** (see below) led the charge to serve gourmet food for affordable prices at an ever-changing series of locations, but now its kin number in the many dozens, clustering in particular on Nicollet Avenue in downtown Minneapolis and on an organized court on Kellogg Boulevard in downtown St. Paul. What follows is a non-comprehensive smattering of the best food carts and food trucks—you can track the evolving scene either on **Heavy Table** (heavytable.com/minneapolis-st-paul-street-food-truck-directory) or the **Minneapolis and St. Paul Street Food Directory** (mspstreetfood.com). The former is more detailed and descriptive, the latter has a search function with a variety of filters. The vast majority of street food purveyors live, die, and convey their location by Twitter, so we've listed Twitter handles for those who would like to track them down.

"Luxury street food" purveyor **Chef Shack** (@chefshack1 on Twitter) deserves a prominent listing here, as its two cosmopolitan owners (Carrie Summer and Lisa Carlson) were doing street food well before it was (locally) cool, building on a background of 40-plus combined years of fine-dining kitchen experience. Famous for the Indian spiced mini doughnuts that have brightened many a farmers' market, Chef Shack also serves up an ever-changing range of delicacies such as "fire tofu" tacos, bison burgers, Lake Superior herring sandwiches, chocolate caramel milk shakes, and more. When the Mill City Farmers market is in season, Chef Shack and its doughnuts are a mainstay. The Shack also brings a homemade condiment bar in tow—half the fun, at least.

Saffron, the downtown Minneapolis restaurant that owns **The World Street Kitchen** (@eatwsk1) food truck, serves high-end Middle Eastern/Mediterranean food, but the food cart has no boundaries. Asian and Latin street food flavors mix and mingle—on any given day you might find short-rib pho, Mexican-style torta sandwich, or a Korean-style "Yum Yum" rice bowl with a soft-cooked egg, peanuts, Chinese broccoli, sesame seeds, and secret sauce. Like most gourmet street food, World Street Kitchen's prices tend to clock in at the $6 to $8 range, and the portion size is typically generous. Homemade beverages like a spiced hibiscus drink add to the truck's appeal.

The **Vellee Deli food** (@VelleeDeli) food truck touts "pan-Asian and Mexican mash-ups" with flavor that's "vellee good!" The truck's mainstay is the Korean bar-becue burrito, a tortilla wrapped around seasoned rice and salsa roja with grilled boneless short ribs and kimchi. The truck also tends to sling quesadillas, tacos (including a battered fish taco pair called The Kraken), and crispy Vellee Roll egg rolls. The truck's young staff are buoyant and entertaining, and only World Street Kitchen and Chef Shack give it a real run for its money in terms of madcap boundary hopping.

NateDogs (@Nate_Dogs) founder Nate Beck had a simple mission in mind when he started his sausage-focused food cart: reinvent the hot dog as something local, flavorful, and upscale. He has succeeded—his snappy natural-casing wieners made with Minnesota-raised meat are superb, particularly when topped with his house-made condiments like mustard made from the beers of local craft-brew superpower Surly Brewing.

The **Saucy Burt's** (@saucyBurts) food cart represents a major departure for founder Sarah Burt—although her professional background is in politics, she has leapt into gastronomy with both feet, cooking at local-goes-avant-garde restaurant Haute Dish and starting up her gourmet meatball sandwich food cart. The subs' moist, flavorful meatballs are a custom blend of pork, beef, and veal, the buns are baked by a local Italian baker, and the tomato sauce has a bright, zesty flavor—it's easily one of the best Italian subs in the area.

The **Dandelion Kitchen** (@dandelionktchn) food truck boasts of its "farm to trailer" food, which includes a variety of simple but classy seasonal eats inspired by whatever happens to be at the market during a given time of year. Charcuterie, roast chicken, grilled cheese, seasonal soup, and other straightforward but elegant meals make this cart a quick way to score a well-balanced lunch. Herb-infused house-made sodas are an added bonus.

The crew at **Hola Arepa** (@holaarepa) doesn't joke around with their seriously Latin-influenced street food. For starters, they're the only local truck slinging *arepas* (dense, crispy cornmeal patties used in lieu of tortillas); on top of that, they incorporate a number of flavor-boosting slow-cooking techniques into their dishes, resulting in delectable slow-roasted pork and pulled chicken-topped *arepa* meals. Before they launched they promised to serve *cuy* (guinea pig), but it is as of this writing not yet a regular part of the truck's menu. For good or ill.

Minnesotans know pasties—these dense Cornish empanada-like stuffed meat pies were the lunch of choice for miners on the Iron Range, a mineral-rich region of the state stretching from Duluth west out to Hibbing and Grand Rapids. **Potter's Pasties** (@potters pasties) has reinvented the dish (normally a simple affair of potatoes, ground beef, and rutabagas—maybe carrots, often gravy) presenting variants including a chicken potpie variant, a pork-and-apple-style pasty, a breakfast pasty (with egg and sausage), and a Thai veggie variety that has most certainly never seen the inside of an iron mine.

Meritage is known as one of the classic French cuisine flagships of St. Paul (or, it could be added, the whole Twin Cities area). So when they jumped into the street food game, it became clear that the craze was likely to be more than a mere passing fad. The **Meritage Crepe Stand** (@meritage_stpaul) dishes up classic crepes with fillings such as Nutella, florentine ham, maple sausage with herbed ricotta—sometimes comforting, sometimes adventurous, but nothing that would seem out of place on the Continent.

The **She Royal truck** (@sheroyalcoco) represents one of the fastest growing segments of Twin Cities dining: East African food. Its veggie sampler with *injera* is a local meat-free favorite, and when the truck has *samosas* on offer, snatch them up.

The **Smack Shack** (@smack_shack) is the post restauranting project (or should that be comeback project?) of Josh Thoma, whose scandal-filled departure from a group of the highest profile restaurants in Minneapolis was the talk of the town in 2010. As improbable as it might seem for a food truck located in a town thousands of miles from the nearest ocean, Smack Shack dishes up lobster rolls that are some of the best-reviewed street food meals in the area, holding up even to their Maine brethren. They're not cheap, but that's a further sign that Thoma is taking his job seriously and buying good product.

The **Waffle Van** (@TheWaffleVan) is the mobile arm of The Bikery Du Nord, a newly established Marine on St. Croix bakery/bike shop/Nordic ski shop triple threat. Unusual for food trucks, the van sells beer, a beverage right in line with its chef-founder's Belgian heritage. Sweet Liege-style Belgian waffles are the van's mainstay.

The story of **Halal Hotdogs** (brianwiley.net/halal-hotdogs) is an intriguing one—the idea of doing an American food (hot dogs) in a halal manner (religiously clean for Muslims) was created by Brian Wiley, an MFA candidate at the Minneapolis College for Art and Design. The project was created as a way to use food to build acceptance for the growing Somali community in Minneapolis-St. Paul; as of this writing, the plan is to run a for-profit hot dog cart as well as a nonprofit hot dog cart that will provide job training for immigrants.

Farm Fresh

The Twin Cities is a metropolitan area swimming in an ocean of farm- and ranchland, with the added bonus of forage-ready wilderness to boot. To the south, there's copious pork (in both Minnesota and Iowa), to the east there's dairy (most notably Wisconsin cheese), to the west there are the proverbial amber waves of grain, and to the north there is the bounty of wild rice, berries, and Lake Superior fish. And in every direction (although, to be fair, more east and south), there's produce in the warm season and overwinter produce via the technological magic of the greenhouse.

Farmers' Markets

Much of the Upper Midwest's farm bounty makes its way to the city in part via more than 50 city-wide and neighborhood-based farmers' markets, many of which have been established over the past decade as interest in farm-to-table dining has boomed, and alternative marketing options—read, the Internet and social media—have made it more feasible for seat-of-the-pants operations to get the word out and attract both buyers and vendors.

What follows are some brief highlights from a few of the farmers' markets around the Cities. If you're in town during market season and can make it out to one of the big ones (Minneapolis or St. Paul), do so—otherwise (or additionally!), you can usually find smaller markets in whatever neighborhood you happen to be staying.

Minneapolis Farmers Market

mplsfarmersmarket.com

The more than 200-member strong Central Minnesota Vegetable Growers Association runs this thriving semi-outdoor market with a primary location at Lyndale and Glenwood Avenues, convenient to downtown Minneapolis, Uptown, and the underserved North section of town. (Another smaller location on Nicollet Mall reaches directly into the heart of downtown.)

The origins of the market date back to an 1876 fruit and vegetable market, and it's one of the two gorillas on the farmers' market scene, distinguished by its red-roofed, open-sided sheds that shelter dozens upon dozens of vendors—230, to be precise, who fill some combination of the 170 available stalls.

Unlike many markets nationwide that only do business 1 or 2 days a week, the Lyndale Market is open 7 days a week from mid-April until mid-November; many vendors continue to sell on winter

Saturdays, and there's a pre-holiday period with trees and other seasonal ornamentals that runs right up to Christmas. (As with any market, it's always best to check the website before you head out if you've got any question about hours, season, or day of week.)

Unlike the more strictly local St. Paul farmers' market, the Minneapolis market does include resellers (grandfathered in from its original origins as a wholesale market) and vendors who offer imported products to help compensate for the region's short growing period. Signage helps shoppers differentiate between local growers and resellers.

Compared to some of the fancier markets (Mill City and Kingfield particularly), the Minneapolis Farmers Market has more of an urban industrial feel to it—the clientele is quite economically diverse (ranging from gourmets on the go to working-class families buying healthy groceries for the week).

The Minneapolis Farmers Market is also host to its own radio show—you can typically catch the Fresh & Local Radio Show at 8 a.m. on Saturday on AM950. The program is hosted by media personality Susan Berkson and locally famous herb grower Bonnie Dehn, and features members of the area food community including farmers and other purveyors—it's a fine way to get up to speed on local agricultural news and community connections.

Parking is fairly plentiful and free, and you should budget about 45 minutes for a thorough exploration of the market.

St. Paul Farmers Market

stpaulfarmersmarket.com

While the main St. Paul Farmers Market is located in the urban Lowertown part of the city, this sprawling octopus of an enterprise includes nearly 20 satellite locations throughout the Twin Cities and surrounding communities.

Established in a two-story brick building in 1853 after a call by the *Minnesota Pioneer* for a farmers' market, the St. Paul Farmers Market has since grown to a 167-stall open-air presence in the heart of the city, operated by the St. Paul Growers' Association, Inc.

The association is strict about who sells at the market, and allows only fresh, locally grown produce to be sold, direct from the grower to the consumer. In addition there are other local products—baked goods, honey, eggs, tasty bagel sandwiches by **Golden's Deli** (p. 162), plants, and other items, including a variety of local meat products.

If you're hoping for a big snapshot of local agriculture or shopping for a complex meal, the St. Paul Farmers Market is the spot to beat—when produce is in season, it's a whirring beehive of activity and fresh food.

The main market season is Saturday and Sunday late April to late November. Parking can be a bit of a challenge when the market's in full swing, but there is a rather extensive free lot available around the corner from the market on East 5th Street and some free spots on East Prince Street as well. Depending on your mood and goals, it's worth allowing 45 minutes to an hour to explore the St. Paul Farmers Market.

Mill City Farmers Market

millcityfarmersmarket.org

Every market has a balance between shop for food/shop for specialty food/look at crafts/nosh like crazy to the point of eating a full breakfast. The Minneapolis and St. Paul Farmers Markets tilt toward number one and number two, somewhat respectively. And while there are farmers with produce present, the downtown Minneapolis–based Mill City Farmers Market is all about the noshing and somewhat about the crafting—its mission is to "support local, sustainable, and organic agriculture, increasing economic opportunities for farmers, urban youth, small businesses, and food artisans," and the result is a lovely riverside stroll under the beneficent gaze of the Guthrie theater and Mill City Museum punctuated by snacking at the many ready-to-eat food vendors at the market.

Founded in 2006 by restaurateur Brenda Langton, Mill City Farmers Market includes some great bites for its guests, including Aunt Else's Aebleskiver (hollow pastry spheres cooked in a special cast-iron pan and stuffed with sweet or savory fillings), the locally renowned shortbread and caramels of Bramblewood Cottage, crepes by Langton's own **Spoonriver** (p. 42), a fine selection of trout products from **Star Prairie Trout Farm** (p. 190), and momos (essentially Tibetan dumplings) from the new but respected restaurant **Gorkha Palace** (p. 80).

If you're serious about shopping and/or agriculture, the big markets may be your best bets, but if you're looking for a lovely walk and an even lovelier breakfast, Mill City is a great pick.

The main market season runs from early May to mid-October. Meter parking is generally available, and the walk from the street over to the market is a pleasant one. Depending on how the crowds are doing and how leisurely your breakfast is, 30 to 45 minutes is a good amount of time to budget for a visit.

Kingfield Farmers Market

kingfieldfarmersmarket.org

For a small market with a neighborhood feel, it's hard to beat the vibrant little Kingfield Farmers Market, which offers a harmonious blend of raw produce, value-add canned and preserved foods, and ready-to-eat treats. The courtyard that it's held in is small, but the well-curated mix of vendors means that visitors can get a lot of bang for their theoretical buck. Highlights include Swede Lake Farm (which reasonably claims to grow the best garlic in the state), the sustainable/diversified farm of Tiny Planet Produce, the complex cave-aged cheeses of Love Tree Farm, the goat cheese of Singing Hills Goat Farm, the delectable doughnuts of **Bogart Loves** (p. 193), the honey and bee–related goods of Bees Kneez and—along with Mill City Farmers Market—Foxy Falafel and local street food veterans **Chef Shack** (p. 199). The market is open every Sunday from late May to late October. Neighborhood street parking is generally available without too much trouble, and 15 to 30 minutes should be ample time to enjoy this little urban gem of a market.

Orchards & Berry Farms

While lacking the fruited bounty of states such as Florida and California, Minnesota does quite well for apples (including a number of state university–engineered varieties such as Honeycrisp and Zestar that have become breakout favorites), berries including strawberries, blueberries, and raspberries, and cold-hardy grapes that make some passable table wines and pleasant dessert wines. Pick-your-own farms dot the countryside convenient to the Twin Cities, but they vary in size and quality.

Minnetonka Orchards offers a wide range of pick-your-own apple trees, plus hay rides, a charming little hobby farm area, and a corn maze designed to appeal to kids. Apple cider doughnuts are the perfect way to start a day of picking from the neatly arranged rows of dwarf apple trees, and while (like the vast majority of pick-your-own farms convenient to the Cities) the prices are no steal versus the grocery store, the overall experience can't be beat—the farm is situated on green rolling hills in the countryside and is well suited for large outdoor events (including weddings, company picnics, etc.). As is the case for all orchards and berry farms, it's best to

THE UNIVERSITY OF APPLES & WINE

An undersung institution that has made a big impact on the world of cold-hardy agriculture, the University of Minnesota is a powerhouse of innovation, pioneering some of the world's most important advances in apple and cold-hardy grape growing. The impact is huge, locally—while Wisconsin wines are still mostly one-note sugar-bombs made from California or other imported grapes, Minnesota wineries have turned out some surprisingly sophisticated and balanced vintages using local grapes that can stand up to the state's tough winters.

Honeycrisp Apple—The surprisingly crisp yet seriously juicy Honeycrisp apple is the university's superstar student, named the State Fruit of Minnesota in 2006. It commands a premium price, and the brand has become famous nationally.

Zestar Apple—An early-season, cold-hardy apple with a long storage life and crisp texture, the Zestar was engineered to cope with early winters and provide a flavor described as having just a touch of brown sugar to it.

SweeTango Apple—The sweet/tart Swee-Tango apple is a direct descendent of the Honeycrisp and Zestar breeds. The university paved new ground from a marketing and copyright perspective with the SweeTango, controversially limiting its production to orchards that were licensed to grow it. (The university learned from a previous hard lesson—according to a grower I spoke to in Bayfield, Wisconsin, bogus Honeycrisps have been a real source of grief for buyers and bona fide Honeycrisp growers alike.)

Frontenac and Frontenac Gris grapes—Introduced in 1996 and 2003 respectively, the Frontenac varieties are disease and cold resistant, and are being planted through the Midwest, New England, and Quebec. The former has a dark, jammy flavor and cherry aroma, the latter a taste of stone fruit with a harmonious balance between fruit and acid. Frontenac Gris lends itself well to dessert and ice wines, both of which can be produced in a colder climate (think Germany, in Europe).

La Crescent grape—As per the U of M website, La Crescent trunks have survived -34°F degree weather and taste intensely of apricot, peach, and citrus, making for high-acid wines that recall Vignoles or Riesling.

Marquette grape—Related to Frontenac and Pinot Noir, Marquette is a cold-hardy red grape introduced in 2006. It's high in sugar and tannins, with notes of cherry and spice.

call ahead the day before and the day of picking to confirm hours and availability of fruit.

Located in Maiden Rock, Wisconsin (a scenic drive from the Cities, and lumped in with nearby Stockholm, Wisconsin as one of our recommended Twin Cities road trips on p. 232), **Rush River Produce** is a local rarity—a working u-pick blueberry farm. In contrast to Maine, for example, Minnesota is not blueberry haven, although the berries are found in some abundance (along with raspberries and serviceberries) around the Lake Superior watershed part of the region. If you laid all of Rush River's blueberry plants out from end to end, you'd have 9 miles of blueberry rows to walk featuring 14 varieties of berries, so there's plenty of fodder for the ambitious picker. As is the case for all pick-your-own farms (see above), a phone call and look at the website to confirm the season is effort well spent.

The Minnesota Department of Agriculture maintains a handy online list pointing to consumer accessible produce farms including strawberry farms: www3.mda.state.mn .us. One of the best is **Apple Jack Orchards** in nearby Delano, Minnesota, which maintains apple trees in addition to a sizable strawberry patch and both fall and summer raspberry patches. There's additional fun stuff for kids including pony rides, an apple cannon and slingshot, a newly added jumping pillow, plus a 5-acre corn maze.

The Farm-to-Fork Movement

For decades, Minneapolis-St. Paul (and cities in Wisconsin and the Dakotas) were a through-the-looking-glass contradiction in terms of eating. Despite being in one of the great agricultural breadbaskets of the nation (Iowa pork, Minnesota turkey, Wisconsin cheese, Dakota grain, and so forth), much of the food served in restaurants was disconnected from a sense of place, while the gems of the region were whisked away to New York or California to be served up as haute cuisines.

As L'Etoile is to Madison, Wisconsin, **Lucia's** (p. 91) is to Minneapolis-St. Paul—one of the pioneering restaurants that got it right fairly early on, incorporating farmers' market finds, seasonality, and local food whenever possible to create food that reflects the terroir of the region. More than a quarter-century old, Lucia's prides itself on a menu heavy on produce (fresh and local whenever possible), lighter entrees, locally sourced meats, and sophisticated-yet-rustic fare such as pates and pickled sides.

Wise Acre Eatery (p. 138), founded by two Lucia's alums, carries forward the ideal of Lucia's with a specific, tandem-operated farm and ranch called Tangletown Gardens in Plato, Minnesota. Cattle, hogs, and chicken come from Tangletown to Wise Acre, accompanied by seasonal produce that enlivens the restaurant's menu in warmer months.

Corner Table (p. 68) built a name for itself as one of the most forward-thinking of the local fare-focused eateries in the Twin Cities. Founded by chef/TV personality/man-about-town Scott

Pampuch, Corner Table has incorporated everything from foraged mushrooms to house-made sodas to exceptional charcuterie and pork belly to distinguish itself from the pack. And while Pampuch (as of this writing) is no longer the restaurant's hands-on chef, Corner Table enjoys a strong reputation among those who love to eat locally and eat well.

No restaurant in the Twin Cities may do as much to quantify and celebrate its connection to the local food scene as **Common Roots** (p. 67) in Uptown, which rigorously audits its own ingredients and menu items to give customers a current running estimate of just how local the menu might be. By owning its reputation with such clarity and ferocity, Common Roots has also endeared itself to many of Uptown's more left-leaning and environmentally conscious residents, who pack its tables to study, meet, work, and eat.

Heartland (p. 148) Chef Lenny Russo is one of the biggest personalities in the Twin Cities food scene, known both for his passion for classic cooking techniques and his loyalty to the local fare that powers his cuisine—his chefs avoid even using olive oil, since the closest Russo could find to local was a supplier in Arkansas. Heartland is immediately adjacent to the excellent and locally driven **St. Paul Farmers Market** (p. 208) and it has its own attached locavore food market that sells value-add products such as pates and charcuterie to guests.

The two locations of **Brasa** (p. 159), the brainchild of Restaurant Alma (p. 39) Chef Alex Roberts, both offer visitors slow-cooked big-batch scratch meals that manage to provide big flavor and a great deal of convenience—that these meals are also made with a heavy emphasis on local food and healthful recipes is a further credit to Roberts, who won Best Chef Midwest in the James Beard Awards in 2010 after a series of previous nominations for the honor.

Numerous other restaurants (**Birchwood,** p. 17, **Spoonriver,** p. 45, and more) also play up their connection to local and seasonal food—the trend seems to be only intensifying as the years go by and Twin Cities chefs gain an appreciation for the bounty in their own backyards.

The Co-op Heartland

There are more cooperative businesses in Minnesota per capita than any other state in the union, and that has a major impact on the world of food, where cooperative grocery stores dot the landscape, and most parts of town have a food co-op to call their own.

Whether that is a direct outgrowth of the Cities' collaborative Scandinavian heritage or their relatively liberal political climate is not entirely clear, but the fact remains: Co-ops are not a fringe movement in Minneapolis and St. Paul; they're a mainstream outlet for locals shopping for their weekly fare. The impact on the local economy is great—co-ops put a premium on buying seasonally and locally, which in turns strengthens local agriculture. The community-first nature of the co-op model also means that food choices tend to be healthier than many conventional grocery stores—whole grains, low- or no-fat alternatives, bulk products, and organic and/or sustainable goods are typically a major part of any given co-op's model.

While co-ops sell memberships (usually for a nominal fee that is quickly recovered through dividends, quarterly savings, and other opportunities), they are open to the general public and are one of the best ways to check out what the local foodshed has to offer in terms of meat, cheese, beverages, and other goods.

The Wedge (2105 S. Lyndale Ave., Minneapolis, MN 55405; 612-871-3993; wedge.coop) is one of the Cities' oldest co-ops, having been founded in a basement by a group of politically and socially conscious neighbors in Minneapolis's Uptown neighborhood in 1974. Its founding values include social justice, sustainable agriculture, health, and the environment, and all of these continue to play out, nearly 40 years later, in the store's commitment to local and organic foods. While the Wedge feels a bit cramped in its current location and its parking lot is famously difficult to navigate, it's a fine place to capture the enduring spirit of the area's local foods movement.

Seward Co-op (2823 E. Franklin Ave., Minneapolis, MN 55406; 612-338-2465; seward.coop), in the Seward Neighborhood of South Minneapolis, stands out along with Linden Hills as one of the newest and sleekest of the bunch. This LEED (Leadership in Energy and Environmental Design)-certified building is equipped with rainwater-capturing architecture and other modifications that minimize its energy use and capitalize on recycled materials. Beyond that, Seward Co-op is notable for wide, well-lit aisles and a friendly, professional  staff—it's more evocative of local luxury grocers like Kowalski's or Lunds than a traditional co-op, which makes do with sometimes spartan conditions.

And the **Mississippi Market** co-ops (at two locations in St. Paul—original location opened in 1979) exert a strong influence on local eaters not just with their wide aisles and diverse selection of products but also with their extensive classes, covering everything from cooking to canning to addressing special dietary needs.

Local Food
(& Beer) Groups

Volunteerism and civic participation is a hallmark of Minnesota and the Twin Cities in general—Minneapolis-St. Paul was found to be the most civically engaged metropolis in the nation in a 2011 report by the National Conference on Citizenship, with (relatively) high levels of trust in government and other civic institutions and a general willingness to get out of the house and collaborate with others on everything from art to politics. Food is no exception—the Twin Cities has a lively culture of clubs, meetups, nonprofits, and other organizations otherwise engaged in the food culture of the area. The tendency to organize and socialize manifests itself in the area's booming co-op scene (see p. 217) but also in a number of other groups; what follows is a mere skim-the-surface sampling of some of the more prominent and/or interesting.

Slow Food Minnesota

slowfoodmn.org

A member of Slow Food International, a global movement with more than 100,000 members that meets locally to, in the words of the group's mission, "create a world in which all people can access and enjoy food that is good for them, good for those who grow it, and good for the planet." The group stages numerous events in the Twin Cities areas, including farm dinners, author readings, gourmet picnics, and more—all are quite affordable and marked by thoughtfulness, an interest in intellectual inquiry, and good eats.

St. Paul Homebrewers Club

sphbc.org

The St. Paul Homebrewers Club is a three-time American Homebrewers Association Club of the Year, in recognition of its members' diligence, skill, and propensity to win national brewing medals and graduate into the world of professional brewing. The club is known locally as being tight-knit and serious-minded—criticism of beers brought to the group is direct, not particularly polite, and can be personally crushing to those wading in unprepared. It's precisely that atmosphere, of course, that leads to its members making leaps and bounds forward in their brewing. Meetings are often held upstairs at the **Happy Gnome,** one of the area's best-regarded beer bars (p. 165).

Institute for Agriculture and Trade Policy

iatp.org

This farm and food policy–focused think tank researches topics as varied as international policymaking institutions such as the World Trade Organization, the toxic chemical BPA in baby bottles, and the plight of small family farms in the Midwest. Locally, the group hosts a wide range of events dealing with contemporary food policy and hot-button current issues. The Institute also founded the acclaimed local coffee roaster and Longfellow neighborhood cafe Peace Coffee in 1996 as the country's first 100 percent certified organic and fair trade coffee company.

Barley's Angels

facebook.com/barleysangelsmn

The world of beer—both production and appreciation—has a reputation for being a man's domain. With the advent of craft brew, it has slowly (and sometimes painfully) become clear that a group representing women in the world of brewing would be a positive force. Thus, Barley's Angels, a nationwide group of individual local chapters dedicated to working with breweries, alehouses, and restaurants to "advance the female consumer craft beer enthusiast." The St. Paul-based Minnesota chapter hosts regular happy hour meetings and brewery tours, the latter being a particularly busy line of work as the Twin Cities brewery scene explodes with new life.

Open Arms of Minnesota

openarmsmn.org

The remarkable nonprofit Open Arms harnesses the power of 1,400 volunteers to cook and delivers free, delicious-by-design meals tailored to meet the nutrition needs of people living with HIV/AIDS, MS, ALS, cancer, and more than 42 other diseases. Operating out of a stunning modern building on Bloomington Avenue in South Minneapolis, the organization is a daily ballet of cooking, packaging, freezing, and delivering meals—more than 400,000 to more than 700 clients in 107 zip codes in 2010 alone. The organization also runs a 2-acre farm called Open Gardens, which produces 15,000 pounds of vegetables a year.

Kindred Kitchen

kindredkitchen.org

Located in Minneapolis's economically challenged North neighborhood, Kindred Kitchen is a vibrant incubator of small, community-based food businesses. By providing high-quality commercial kitchen space, workshops, guidance to obtain proper licensing, insurance and other certifications, and a network of like-minded entrepreneurs, Kindred Kitchen helps small local businesses plan their route to success and get off the ground. Its initial impact has been felt by the growing food truck and food cart scene in the Twin Cities, where a place to prep food and a firm grounding in marketing and pricing can make all the difference between success and failure.

Urban farmers

Not an organized group per se, but a community worth knowing about—new ordinance changes in Minneapolis and a resurgence of interest in growing wholesome food has led to a notable uptick in city folk turning gardens, backyards, and even large vacant lots into food-producing systems capable of turning out hundreds of pounds of vegetables, berries, chicken eggs, and more. If you do a web search for Minneapolis urban farmers, you'll stumble upon profiles of some of the better known and more ambitious members of the informal brotherhood, and there's an organization called **Harvest Moon Backyard Farmers** (harvestmoon farmers.blogspot.com) that will help you transform your own garden into a working urban food mini-farm.

Chefs for Change and People Serving People

peopleservingpeople.org/events/chefs.php

The monthly Chefs for Change event is a dinner party with a purpose—it brings together high-end chefs, 30 to 40 generous members of the community, and a cause—helping People Serving People, an organization that provides emergency housing and community services for homeless families in Minneapolis.

Food Fests
& Events

The **Bayfield Apple Festival** (bayfield.org/festivals_events_ apple_festival.php) on the South Shore of Lake Superior is a bit of a drive from the Twin Cities, but thousands make the pilgrimage each year to this little town on the banks of a big lake. The early October apple festival typically brings about 50,000 people to Bayfield (population 611), where they gather to sample from hundreds of food and craft booths, shop for art, enjoy music and apple pie contests, and eat traditional fish boil dinners. Pick-your-own orchards and a boat parade are part of the fun. See the South Shore road trip (p. 236) for more information on this Twin Cities–accessible destination.

Wisconsin may have the national reputation for beer thanks to the ancient and mostly extinct beer giants of Milwaukee, but Minnesota holds its own these days with a rapidly expanding craft brew community. A number of different festivals put beer first. The

City Pages Beer Festival (citypages.com) in June brings together dozens of breweries sampling hundreds of beers. In March, **Firkin Fest at the Happy Gnome** (thehappygnome.com) celebrates cask-conditioned beer, with as many as 80 different varieties available for the hundreds upon hundreds of attendees. It's crowded, but a beer-lover's delight. And **Schell's Bock Fest** (schellsbrewery.com) isn't for the meek of heart—this outdoor festival takes place at the New Ulm, Minnesota, brewery somewhere between late February and early March, a time of year still cold enough to fall squarely in the heart of Minnesota's nationally famous brutal winter. This German-style Mardi Gras celebration features steins full of caramel-colored bock beer, and the option to have your beer "poked" with a red-hot wrought-iron poker, which foams up the brew and imparts a smoky, caramelized flavor. It also features colorful and sometimes nicely toasted guests (many of whom have been bused in from the Twin Cities), so be aware that this isn't your typical brewfest.

Brewing powerhouse Surly sponsors an annual event called **Surlyfest** (surlybrewing.com), which features live music, food vendors, and copious amounts of the brewery's high-octane, highly creative beer. Another (perhaps even more eagerly anticipated) Surly event is **Darkness Day,** typically held in October. Inspired by Dark Lord Day at Indiana's Three Floyds Brewing, Darkness Day is the brewery's annual release of its Darkness beer, a dark, heavy, palate-crushing, expensive, high-gravity brew that locals line up for. Reviewer Adam Garcia, writing on Beer Advocate (where the beer merited an overall "A" grade) wrote: "Big and bold. Milk chocolate. Sweet coffee and cream. Lovely roasted flavors. Over-ripe fruits.

Hops come through late and balance all the sweet flavors with a little bitterness. No discernible heat despite the abv. Quite complex . . . I had high expectations and they were met, if not exceeded."

If you don't know what an *eelpout* is and you don't love cold-weather partying, then the **Annual International Eelpout Festival** (heavytable.com/the-redemption-of-the-eel-pout) on Leech Lake in Walker, Minnesota, may not be for you. Established in 1979, the festival is a celebration of ice fishing, the drinking of enormous quantities of affordable beers, brutally cold temperatures, and, first and foremost, the ugly, much-disrespected fish called the eelpout. Every ice fishing shack becomes a party house, and more than 10,000 attend the event in order to drink, dance, play cribbage, and eat some eelpout. The fatty eelpout (properly called a burbot, but also known as a lawyer fish) is typically fried up into small nuggets, but it can also be pan-roasted to good effect.

The **Minneapolis-St. Paul Zombie Pub Crawl** (zombiepub-crawl.com) got its start in 2005, when 150 locals donned zombie gear and staggered from pub to pub in Northeast Minneapolis. It has since grown to a more than 20,000-zombie-strong festival of music, beer, and food operating in both of the Twin Cities, booking national acts, and ferrying its undead horde from city to city on party buses. Among the select community of citywide zombie pub crawls, it has a distinguished national reputation as both the first and biggest of its kind.

Febgiving: A Holiday of Sweet Mercy

Name a reason that Minneapolis-St. Paul is an undesirable place to live. What's that? Yes, winter. The Twin Cities boast the nation's best literacy rate, a high rate of physical fitness, strong education and health care, a beautiful parks system, a relatively low rate of crime, a thriving cultural scene, and a booming local food community—only winter keeps them from being paradise on Earth. (Some of course would insist that only winter could keep the riff-raff out, but that's a debatable point.)

Winter's first 2 or 3 months are easy. The quick procession of Halloween, Thanksgiving, and Christmas/Hannukah keep spirits bright and cheery, and snow feels like a gift, not a curse, when it's making the holidays merry. New Year's Eve is inevitably a blast, and that week or two afterward is a welcome rest and respite from the madcap socializing and outdoor partying that mark the onset of winter.

And then . . . things sort of grind to a halt. With nothing to look forward to except for the distant advent of spring (late March at best, late April more typically, mid-May under really bad conditions),

Numerous local publications have their own food events every year—look in particular for the **Minnesota Monthly Food & Wine Show** (foodwineshow.com) in early March and the **Mpls.St. Paul Taste!** festival (mspmag.com/dining) in late September/early October. Both feature samples, demonstrations, classes, and a mix between a trade show and sip-and-sample atmosphere. Tickets are typically at or above $65 a person.

people get more withdrawn and moody, and shoveling the snow goes from fun to exercise to torture. Valentine's Day tends to add to the problem.

Thus: Febgiving, a festival of hope in a time of dire emotional straits. Held the Saturday night in February on or just before Valentine's Day, the rules are simple: You put together a full-court press Thanksgiving meal and invite your friends. The result is a mid-winter fest of cheer and goodwill, fueled by turkey, pies, sausage stuffing, pumpkin trifle, hard cider, local beer, and whatever else can be laid hold of or created to order. The holiday (which, it must be disclosed, was created by myself and my wife) has been covered in depth by both the *Star Tribune* and the local CBS affiliate, WCCO, and may well in coming years become a local custom of some prominence.

Or perhaps not. Either way, it exists as a way out of winter gloom for those not afraid to heat up the house with some festive cooking and baking, and for those not afraid to tackle the mountains of dishes left by dozens of departing friends and family members. All things considered, it's preferable to snow shoveling.

The **Minnesota State Fair** (mnstatefair.org) runs from late August to Labor Day and is more than just a food event, of course, what with the national-level acts, stumping politicians, and extensive midway. But for many visitors, food is king. See p. 24 for a rundown of the extensive and ever-changing spread.

Pungent odor aside, the **Minnesota Garlic Festival** in Hutchinson, Minnesota (sfa-mn.org/garlicfest), is one of the state's most beloved gastronomic traditions, featuring more than 100 varieties of garlic, bands, a wine tasting, high-profile local chefs, a kids' kite-flying attraction, and old-fashioned picnic games.

A Germanic tradition and love of good brew means that late September through early October is studded with **Oktoberfest** drink specials, beer gardens, and special events. Local German restaurants lead the way—look to the **Black Forest Inn** (p. 18) in Minneapolis (which has a 10-day version of the celebration) and the **Glockenspiel** (p. 146) in St. Paul for Oktoberfest festivities.

Arborfest (held on campus at Macalester in St. Paul) features craft beers, wine samplings, food, music, and a raffle. The event benefits the Family Tree Clinic (familytreeclinic.org), a local organization that works to cultivate health through sexual health care and education.

Smaller festivals tap into the fringe of local food culture: **Gastro Non Grata** (gastronongrata.blogspot.com) is a local ongoing event series that pairs up popular local bands with hot local chefs and creates food/beer/music jam sessions that are eagerly attended. (The event describes itself as "a local chef-driven, alcohol-fueled music machine.") The Heavy Table's **North Coast Nosh** (heavytable.com) is a bit more sedate—it's an ongoing events series that gathers local purveyors. Brewers, cheesemakers, beekeepers, bakers, and more all gather and sample their wares for ticket holders.

Three Upper Midwestern Foodie Road Trips

The dignified prairie isolation that is the very quality that gives Minneapolis-St. Paul its considerable charm is also what can make the metropolis challenging for newcomers. Recent transplants from the East Coast, used to being able to make 4-hour hops from Boston to New York to Washington, DC, suddenly find themselves with seemingly nowhere to go—the charming little city of Madison is a full 4 hours away on the highway, and Chicago closer to 6½ hours' drive. The good news is that while other cities aren't necessarily easily accessible, there are a few charming road trips convenient from the Twin Cities that combine good food and natural beauty.

Stockholm, WI

An hour and a half from the Cities

Ask a local about Stockholm, WI, and there's a 50/50 chance they'll respond by saying, "Oh, the Pizza Farm?" If the idea of sitting in the grass on a farm eating brick-oven baked pizza rich with house-grown toppings appeals to you, it might be worth a pilgrimage out to the **A to Z Produce Pizza Farm** (N2956 Anker Lane, Stockholm, WI 54769; no phone; atozproduceandbakery.com), which is open only on Tuesday nights from 4:30 to 8 during the summer. Lines can get crazy at this restaurant/farm/weekly festival—it's not unusual for hundreds of orders to be put in, and though the oven can churn out a pizza a minute when it gets cruising, a certain amount of bucolic idling is part of the experience. It's a good idea to bring your own wine or beer, picnic blanket, and chairs if you're not a sit-in-the-grass type person.

If the Pizza Farm's an experience, then Stockholm proper is a feeling. Nestled into the shore of Lake Pepin (a particularly wide bulge in the Mississippi River), Stockholm sits at the terminus of a particularly lovely drive from the cities, featuring twists and turns, valleys and streams, and some steep country hillsides.

The village of Stockholm recalls a New England seaside town, minus the clams and lobster—while there's a backbone of year-round residents, the tiny downtown is made to be welcoming to tourists. Within a few square blocks, the village offers antiques shops, a well-stocked food store specializing in Wisconsin specialty foods, a cooking store, free-to-borrow bicycles for rural touring, a few restaurants, and a regionally legendary pie shop.

The **Stockholm Pie Company** (N2030 Spring St., Stockholm, WI 54769; 715-442-5505; stockholmpiecompany .com) has gained such a strong regional reputation that it has become a draw unto itself. The carefully crafted house-made pies are invariably excellent, their berry pies deftly balancing sweet and tart flavors, and their autumn pies managing to capture the taste of the fruit or squash without being too austere. You can have a slice and a cup of coffee on-site, and/or buy a whole pie for consumption later.

If you've never thought about artisanal cider, now's a good time to start—Stockholm is home to the **Maiden Rock Winery & Cidery** (W12266 King Lane, Stockholm, WI 54769; 715-448-3502; maidenrockwinerycidery.com), which uses a wide variety of heirloom and otherwise unusual apple varieties to make its potent potables. Should you find yourself road-tripping at the start of winter, the Cidery does an annual December medieval feast and Wassailing of the Apple Trees that is a visual and gastronomic spectacle unique to the region.

And should you be in Stockholm on a Friday evening, **Gelly's Pub and Eatery** (W12128 State Hwy. 35, Stockholm, WI 54769; 715-442-2023; gellyspub.com) does as credible—and reasonably priced—a Wisconsin fish fry as you can find throughout the state. Condiments are made in house, and the fish is crispy, not greasy.

If you're planning a full-on road trip to Stockholm, just keep your eye on the calendar, as many businesses are only open during the warmer months of late spring through mid-autumn, and only on weekend or weekend-ish (Wednesday, Thursday, Friday) days of the week.

Duluth & the North Shore

Two and a half hours from the Cities

The strange, San Francisco-esque hills-on-the-water city of Duluth is one of the most common warm-weather destinations for Minneapolitans and St. Paulites, if only because of its gateway status—from Duluth you can easily access the rest of the North Shore of Lake Superior and its myriad hiking, fishing, camping, and dining opportunities.

Duluth itself shouldn't be overlooked, however—there are a number of interesting things going on with the Duluth food scene that deserve a closer look. First and foremost may be the local food gone elegantly upscale at **Northern Waters Smokehaus** (DeWitt-Seitz Marketplace, 394 Lake Ave. S, Suite 106, Duluth, MN 55802; 218-724-7307; northernwaterssmokehaus.com). Northern Waters carefully smokes its salmon, its Lake Superior whitefish, and its Lake Superior lake trout and uses the resulting product to assemble some of the best sandwiches available in the Upper Midwest. The Cajun Finn (house smoked Cajun salmon, green onion cream cheese, roasted red peppers, pepperoncini, and lettuce on stirato) is one of the house favorites, and as good a lunch as you can find anywhere. That Northern Waters also does nationally regarded charcuterie (including more challenging aged, fermented meats such as salami) is an added attraction.

Farther up the Shore, in Knife River, **Russ Kendall's Smokehouse** (149 Scenic Dr., Lake No. 2, MN 55609; 218-834-5995; facebook.com/RussKendalls) is a much more traditional joint with many decades of history on the Shore, and is even fussier than Northern Waters about using local fish—its only imported fish is Alaskan salmon. While a favorite stop for tourists, it's the locals who queue up here even on off-season weekdays to get their ration of smoked fish.

In Duluth proper, visitors curious about Scandinavian food may enjoy the newly established **Takk for Maten Cafe** (11 East Superior St., Suite 110, Duluth, MN 55802; 218-464-1260; facebook.com/Takk4matencafe), which brings together traditions such as open-faced sandwiches and Swedish pancakes (*lefse*) with innovations like *lefse* dogs and *lefse* sandwiches.

Farther north in Grand Marais, visitors are well advised to try some (extremely) fresh Lake Superior fish at the deeply environmentally friendly and locally conscious **Angry Trout Cafe** (416 MN 61, Grand Marais, MN 55604; 218-387-1265; angrytroutcafe.com). Local produce and fish brought in next door at the Dockside Fish Market make this a meal to remember. If herring are in season, try one grilled—it's mind-blowingly tasty.

Homespun desserts also pop up throughout the shore—from chocolates to doughnuts to pie, there's really no sweet craving that can't be satisfied. A couple of the best options: the **World's Best Donuts** (10 E. Wisconsin St., Grand Marais, MN 55604; 218-387-1345; worldsbestdonutsmn.com) in Grand Marais (surely an overstatement, but not by all that much), and the **Rustic Inn** (218-834-2488) in Castle Danger, MN, which turns out one of the best commercially made pecan pies in the region. Skip Betty's Pies if you see it—it has gone from North Shore standard to heavily commercialized money-making tourist attraction.

The South Shore

Three and a half hours from the Cities

If the North Shore is the rustic gateway to the great North Woods and the wilds of Lake Superior, the South Shore is the cozy, civilized alternative. Visitors swarm the area (which is roughly composed of the alphabetically memorable cities of Ashland, Bayfield, and Cornucopia) for the annual **Bayfield Apple Festival** (bayfield.org/festivals_events_apple_festival.php), which sees crowds numbering in the tens of thousands. Bayfield's history as an apple stronghold comes from its sheltered position on the Lake (the Apostle Islands help moderate the weather), and its proximity to the islands makes it

a great jumping-off point for further adventures including kayaking the islands' sea caves, or a ferry trip for a drink at **Tom's Burned Down Cafe** on Madeline Island (234 Middle Rd., La Pointe, WI 54850; 715-747-6100; tomsburneddowncafe.com). The Burned Down Cafe is actually a burned-down cafe, partially reconstructed with tents and trailers.

The **Rittenhouse Inn** in Bayfield (301 Rittenhouse Ave., Bayfield, WI 54814; 888-561-4667; rittenhouseinn.com) makes for a stately base of operations in the area—this professionally run bed-and-breakfast is based in two elegant and well-maintained mansions. Defiantly low tech (you won't find Wi-Fi or televisions), the Rittenhouse is made for guests who actually want to unplug and relax, and it features a restaurant that does a nice upscale supper and a rip-roaringly good continental breakfast.

Maggie's (257 Manypenny Ave., Bayfield, WI 54814; 715-779-5641; maggies-bayfield.com) in Bayfield serves an eclectic mix of Tex-mex favorites and local fare including the delicious if slightly dangerous-sounding fried whitefish livers (think a lighter, more elegant spin on classic liver and onions). It's the best sort of spot to hit in a tourist-friendly town like Bayfield—it's typically busy with locals and visitors alike.

Judy's Gourmet Garage (85130 Hwy. 13, Bayfield, WI 54814; 715-779-5365) in Bayfield may be the only commercial pie maker that can give **Stockholm Pie Co.** (p. 233) a real run for its money. Located in a residential home's honest-to-goodness garage, the Gourmet Garage is the number one go-to spot for apple pie, the area's specialty.

Lovers of good brew and good food are advised to pop down to Ashland to sample the offerings of the **Deep Water Grille** and **South Shore Brewery** (808 W. Main St.; Ashland, WI 54806; 715-682-4200; southshorebrewery.com). This brewpub is deeply in touch with local food and has gone so far as to source its grain and hops locally as much as is possible. The product (both food and drink) is top-notch, and the Brewery serves as a bustling center of social life in the quaint lakeside town of Ashland.

Recipes

Although Minneapolis and St. Paul are nationally known for their Scandinavian and Germanic heritage, both cities are melting pots, with visitors and residents from all over the world. Sizable populations with Southeast Asian, Middle Eastern, and African heritage have left their culinary imprint on the area, and the fare at local restaurants starts with local farm produce and dairy products and travels to destinations both distant and exotic. The following recipes represent that geographic diversity and present just a taste of the local flavor.

Spiced Lamb & Mejdool Date Tagine

Guests flock to Saffron for its small-plate-style riffs on Middle Eastern and North African food. This tagine is one of the richest and most celebratory dishes from Saffron's repertoire.

Tagine is a type of dish found in the North African cuisines of Algeria, Morocco, and Tunisia, and is named after the special pot in which it is cooked. They are slow-cooked stews braised at low temperatures, resulting in tender meat with aromatic vegetables and sauce. If you don't have a tagine pot, this recipe could also be prepared in a covered baking dish or cast-iron pot.

Serves 8

- 1 lamb shoulder, deboned and cut into 6 pieces (about 5 pounds)
- 3 tablespoons Spice Trail Tagine Spice* or 1 tablespoon each smoked paprika, cumin, and cayenne, blended
- Salt to taste
- ¼ cup vegetable oil or ghee**
- 3 tablespoons vegetable oil
- 6 garlic cloves, sliced thin
- 2 large onions, chopped
- 8 carrots, peeled and sliced
- 4 large tomatoes, chopped
- 3 cups rich chicken stock
- 3 cups cooked chickpeas (not canned)
- ¼ cup fresh chopped cilantro
- ¼ cup fresh chopped flat-leaf parsley
- 1½ cup sliced mejdool dates
- 1 preserved lemon, sliced thin
- 3 tablespoons lemon juice

* *Spice Trail spice blends can be ordered online from SaffronMpls.com*

** *Ghee is a form of preserved butter available in Middle Eastern or Indian grocery stores*

In a large bowl mix the lamb shoulder with 2 generous tablespoons of the spice blend, salt, and 3 tablespoons of vegetable oil, making sure to coat thoroughly with spices. Cover and refrigerate for 1 hour at least.

Heat remaining oil/ghee in tagine or large cast-iron pot and place lamb in 1 layer without overcrowding the pan then sear on all sides. Remove meat from tagine and place garlic, onions, carrots, tomatoes, and remaining spice blend then cook on low heat. Add chicken stock and return lamb to tagine, cover and place in oven at 300°F. Bake for 2 to 3 hours and then add the chickpeas, cilantro, parsley, mejdool dates, preserved lemon and lemon juice. Cover and let stand for 10 minutes before serving.

Courtesy of Chef Sameh Wadi of Saffron Restaurant and World Street Kitchen (p. 200)

Ginger Duck Gyoza with Ponzu Plum Sauce (Japanese Pot Stickers)

Like most of the food at Masu Sushi and Robata, these Japanese pot stickers walk the line between hearty bar food and exquisite little packages of flavor. They're both elegantly balanced and utterly inhalable.

Makes about 50 pieces

1 package Japanese gyoza skins (about 50 per pack)

Cornstarch for dusting

Gyoza Filling

1 pound ground duck (chicken or pork can be substituted)

12 ounces napa cabbage (about ¼ large head)

½ teaspoon plus 1 teaspoon Kosher salt (cut salt in half if using table salt)

½ teaspoon fresh ground pepper

3 tablespoons soy sauce

2 tablespoons sake rice wine

2 scallions

2 cloves garlic, minced

2 teaspoons minced ginger

Chef's note: *Get duck from your local butcher. They may even be able to butcher or even grind it for you, or try your hand at breaking down a whole duck. Here is a hint; the technique is the same as a chicken or a turkey. If duck is not your style, try ground chicken or pork. When you have the duck meat ready, keeping it very cold, use either a grinder or a heavy-duty mixer to grind the meat or chop it, skin and fat included, until it looks like ground meat.*

For the Filling: *Chop napa cabbage to a small dice. Take 1 teaspoon kosher salt and mix with the chopped napa cabbage and set aside for at least 20 minutes.*

Meanwhile take the remaining salt, pepper, soy sauce, and sake and mix together. Slice the scallions into fine rings. Add the minced garlic and ginger to the soy-sake mix with the scallions. Using a strainer, squeeze out as much water as possible from the cabbage. Discard water. Add the cabbage and soy-sake mix to cold ground duck and gently mix. Keep cold.

Gyoza Plum Dipping Sauce

1 ½ cups Japanese ponzu sauce

3 tablespoons Neri Ume sauce (Japanese plum and red Shiso sauce; or if not available substitute 3 tablespoons extra plum sauce)

6 tablespoons Chinese plum sauce

3 tablespoons Asian chili oil

Whisk together first 3 ingredients. Next, add chili oil and mix gently. The chili oil will float on top.

To Form the Gyoza

Chef's note: *Start by gathering 5 to 6 friends. When I lived in Japan Gyoza were made as a social act. Make sure everyone has a teaspoon and a small bowl of water. And then, let the social act begin!*

Bring a large pot of water to boil. Line a cookie sheet with wax paper and lightly dampen a towel to cover the gyoza as they are prepared.

Take a teaspoon of mix at a time and put it in the center of one sheet of gyoza. Using your finger, dip it in a small bowl of water and dampen the edge of the skin. Fold skin in half, being careful not to get the filling on the edges. Pleat the edges, making a "Z" fold about 5 to 7 times in each gyoza. This may take a little practice.

After all the gyoza are made, in stages boil the gyoza for 4–6 minutes until tender like pasta. Place on another cookie sheet dusted with cornstarch. When all the gyoza have been boiled, warm a small amount of oil in 2 large sauté pans. Brown the bottoms of the gyoza.

Traditionally gyoza are dusted with a large amount of cornstarch on the bottom to help them stick together. If you would like to try this, use more cornstarch and just after placing the gyoza in the pan very tightly together CAREFULLY add a few tablespoons of water in the pan. Use a lid to avoid splashing oil and make sure the pan is not too hot. The cornstarch will dissolve in the water and later connect all the gyoza.

To Serve

Gyoza are best served family style. Serve the dipping sauce in small bowls for each guest. Garnish with sliced scallion. Enjoy.

Courtesy of Executive Chef Alex Chase of Masu Sushi & Robata (p. 96)

Harvest Pumpkin Soup

St. Paul's Meritage restaurant marries classic rustic French cuisine with local ingredients to make a satisfying array of dishes that enchant with their warmth and depth. This harvest pumpkin soup is one of the restaurant's autumn signatures.

Chef's note: *This recipe is the most requested in my repertoire. People love to know that it's based on my mother's recipe. Greg Reynolds at Riverbend Farms grows a whole field of pumpkin for me each year just for this soup.*

Serves 8

4 each sugar pumpkins
½ pound butter, melted
1 cup brown sugar, packed
2 tablespoons ground cinnamon
2 teaspoons ground nutmeg
¼ teaspoon mace
5 each shallots thinly sliced
½ onion, sliced thin

1 stalk celery
1 carrot
3 garlic cloves
1 cup sherry wine
2 quarts vegetable stock
2 cups heavy cream
Salt and pepper to taste

Cut the pumpkin in half and brush with ½ of the butter and ½ of the spices and sugar. Place on a cookie sheet and roast in a 350°F oven until tender. Allow to cool slightly and remove the skin.

In a large stock pot add the remaining butter over medium heat and cook the vegetables until tender, but not brown. Add the sherry and reduce by half.

Add the roasted pumpkin and all the remaining ingredients and simmer for 20 minutes.

Place the soup in a blender or food processor (a blender will yield a smoother consistency) and carefully puree the soup.

You can garnish the soup with nuts, whipped cream, or crème frâiche.

Courtesy of Chef Russell Klein of Meritage (p. 151)

Rhubarb Ratafia Ketchup

The field- and forage-driven cooking of writer and cook Brett Laidlaw celebrates the seasonal bounty of the Upper Midwest. Like most of Laidlaw's recipes, this rhubarb ratafia ketchup is deceptively simple, turning local wholesome flavors into an elegant package of flavor.

Chef's note: The springtime garden is often generous to a fault with its rhubarb, and there are only so many strawberry-rhubarb pies one can eat. For 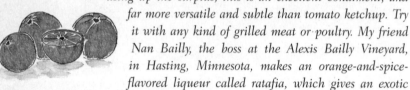 using up the surplus, this is an excellent condiment, and far more versatile and subtle than tomato ketchup. Try it with any kind of grilled meat or poultry. My friend Nan Bailly, the boss at the Alexis Bailly Vineyard, in Hasting, Minnesota, makes an orange-and-spice-flavored liqueur called ratafia, which gives an exotic tinge to the ketchup. The ketchup will keep for several weeks in the fridge, and can be frozen, as well.

If you don't have or can't find ratafia, substitute port for the ratafia, and combine the port and cider vinegar in a saucepan along with 2 strips of orange zest removed with a vegetable peeler, 1 whole clove, and 1 point of star anise. Bring to a boil, remove from heat, cover, and let steep for 1 hour. Strain out and discard the orange peel and spices. Add the infused liquid to rhubarb, etc., and proceed as above.

Makes 2 pints

2 pounds rhubarb stalks, cut into ½-inch pieces
⅓ cup ratafia
¼ cup apple cider vinegar

1 cup sugar
¼ teaspoon salt
Pinch cayenne pepper

In a medium saucepan, combine the rhubarb with the ratafia, vinegar, sugar, and salt. Bring to a boil and cook briskly until the rhubarb pieces wilt into the liquid. Turn the heat to low, cover the saucepan, and simmer, stirring often, until the rhubarb falls apart, about 10 minutes. Rhubarb can vary greatly in its—what's the word?—viscosity, perhaps. If your ketchup seems too thick, add a bit of water, so it flows. Add cayenne pepper to taste. For a smoother texture, you can purée the finished ketchup in a blender or food processor.

Courtesy of Brett Laidlaw of the blog and book *Trout Caviar*

Pork Pate with
Hen of the Woods Mushroom

The impact of European cuisine made local can be strongly felt in Minneapolis and St. Paul when you taste local charcuterie, which brings the Upper Midwest's Germanic meat processing tradition together with products from ranchers and hunters. This pork pate unites ground pork with the flavorful hen of the woods mushroom, which can be foraged in the wild.

2½ pounds ground pork (a small amount of liver in this mix is always good)

1 tablespoon shallot, chopped

½ cup parsley

1 tablespoon garlic, chopped

2 tablespoons salt

1½ tablespoons sugar

1 tablespoon rillete spice (equal parts white pepper, allspice, nutmeg, cinnamon, ginger, and coriander)

1 teaspoon pink salt or Insta cure #1

½ tablespoon ground ginger

½ cup cream

2 eggs

2 tablespoons all-purpose flour

½ pound sautéed hen of the woods mushroom, chopped and cooled

1 pound caul fat or 1 pound pancetta

Mix the meat and seasonings in a chilled mixer bowl with a chilled paddle attachment for 2 minutes. Add cream, eggs, flour, and mushroom and mix until combined. Taste by cooking a small amount in gently boiling water. Adjust whatever seasonings you like. Line a terrine pan with caul fat if you can get it or strips of pancetta. Pack the mixture in tight so there are no air bubbles.

Put a lid on the terrine pan and bake to 145°F in a water bath in a 350°F oven.

Let the terrine cool and then press it with a weight overnight in the refrigerator.

Unmold the following day. Slice and enjoy with baguette and mustard and pickles.

Courtesy of Mike Phillips of the Three Sons Meat Co.

Chèvre Cheesecake

Goat cheese cheesecake is typical of the high-flying fare of Porter & Frye's downtown Minneapolis operation— it's sophisticated and indulgent, harnessing Minnesota cheese in service of cosmopolitan flavor. The restaurant's bison Reuben accomplishes a similar goal on the savory side, serving up local buffalo meat in a globally recognized package.

Chef's note: *The chèvre cheesecake also stemmed from my desire to eat local. The chevre comes from Donnay in Kimball, Minnesota. The grassy tartness of the chèvre lends itself nicely to desserts. I serve it with a sour cherry compote.*

Yields 1 8-inch round pan

Graham Cracker Crust

2 cups graham cracker crumbs   4 ounces unsalted butter, melted

Filling

8 ounces cream cheese, room temperature

8 ounces Donnay chevre

9 ounces sour cream

6½ ounces sugar

1 teaspoon vanilla extract

1½ eggs

2 egg yolks

2 ounces heavy cream

Preheat oven to 325°F.

Combine the crumbs and butter. Pack into the bottom of your pan.

Combine in a mixer with a paddle attachment cream cheese, chèvre, sour cream, sugar, and vanilla.

Mix with the paddle on medium speed until smooth.

Turn the mixer to low and slowly pour in the eggs and yolks. Mix until combined.

Add the cream; mix until combined.

Strain through a fine-mesh sieve.

Pour into the pan and bake 35–40 minutes in a water bath.

Courtesy of Chef Sarah Master of Porter & Frye (p. 112)

Bison Reuben

Chef's note: *The Bison Reuben comes from my search for the perfect Reuben. It is my favorite sandwich! Of course, I love to use local ingredients, so I purchase my bison from Northstar Farm in Rice Lake, Wisconsin. The cabbage comes from Dragsmith in Barron, Wisconsin. Nothing makes me happier than my favorite sandwich being made with local ingredients. It's a huge seller on our lunch menu. It provides the guest with a familiar item using an exotic ingredient (bison).*

Serves 6

- 2¼ pounds corned bison brisket, shaved (recipe follows)
- 3 cups pickled cabbage (recipe follows)
- 6 slices Swiss cheese
- 12 slices rye bread
- 1 pint thousand island dressing (recipe follows)

Preheat the broiler.

On a cookie sheet, make 6 piles of bison brisket. Top it with the cabbage, then the slices of cheese on top of that.

Place under the broiler until the cheese is melted and the brisket is warm.

In the meantime, toast the bread and spoon some thousand island onto it.

Using an offset spatula, transfer each pile onto slices of bread.

Close up the sandwiches, slice in half, and serve.

Thousand Island

2 cups mayo
1 cup minced baby pickles
5 cloves garlic, minced
¼ cup minced chives
¼ cup ketchup
2 teaspoons sugar

Mix everything together.

Pickled Cabbage

½ yellow onion, julienned
3 cloves garlic, sliced
1 head red cabbage, julienned
⅓ cup sherry vinegar
⅓ cup apple cider vinegar
½ cup white wine
1 pint chicken stock
1 bay leaf
2 teaspoons caraway seeds
⅓ cup honey
Salt to taste

In a large pot over medium heat, sweat the onions until translucent.

Stir in the garlic and the cabbage, cook for 3 minutes until cabbage is starting to soften.

Add everything else and bring to a simmer. Cook over medium heat, stirring frequently, until the cabbage is very soft and most of the liquid has evaporated, about 1 hour.

Season with salt to taste.

Corned Bison Brisket

Pickling Spices

¼ cup whole black peppercorns

¼ cup mustard seeds

¼ cup whole coriander

¼ cup red pepper flakes

¼ cup whole allspice

2 cinnamon sticks

¼ cup crushed bay leaves

¼ cup whole cloves

2 tablespoons ground ginger

Mix everything together.

For the Brisket

½ gallon water

2 cups kosher salt

½ cup sugar

1 head garlic, halved

½ cup pickling spices (see above)

¾ gallon ice

1 bison brisket, preferably from Northstar Farm

Put everything but the ice and brisket into a large pot.

Bring to a boil, stirring occasionally until the salt and sugar have dissolved.

Remove from heat and stir in the ice. When brine is cooled completely, put the brisket in and let sit in the brine in the cooler for 5 days.

After 5 days, remove brisket from the brine and put in a large pot with 1 gallon of water and another ½ cup of pickling spice. Bring to a boil, reduce to a simmer and cook until the brisket is no longer tough, about 6 hours.

Remove from the liquid, allow to cool, and thinly slice for Reubens.

Courtesy of Chef Sarah Master of Porter & Frye (p. 112)

Dingle Fish Pie

The Pilrain brothers of Patriots Tavern and Roma Restaurant work their culinary wonders by ensuring that their restaurants bring in a coherent, exotic suite of flavors—from New England and from Italy, respectively. These two recipes are both transportive and representative of what you'll find at Patriots Tavern and Roma.

Chef's note: Dingle is a small fishing town on the southern tip of Ireland's coast. There are many variations for this recipe, but I love the simplicity and richness of this one. Many recipes have mashed potatoes on top similar to shepherd's pie, but I enjoy the crust of buttered breadcrumbs and cheese on top with Yukon gold potatoes in the dish. The true spelling would be Dinglefish Pie. I guess smashing the words together makes for one great question for many (what the heck is Dinglefish?) so we opted to go with the above. This dish has become a Patriot Tavern specialty, so here it is!

Serves 4

2 tablespoons cooking oil

1 tablespoon unsalted butter

12 jumbo shrimp (peeled and deveined)

12 ounces fresh salmon (cut into 12 1-ounce pieces)

12 large sea scallops (side muscle removed)

Salt and pepper to taste

1½ pounds Yukon gold potatoes (blanched and cut into 1-inch cubes)

6 ounces sherry wine

2 cups Alfredo sauce

1 cup shredded cheddar

1 cup shredded parmesan

1½ cups panko (Japanese white bread crumbs)

Heat oil and butter in large sauté pan. add shrimp, salmon, and scallops to pan, seasoning both sides with salt and pepper. Sear both sides and add the potatoes to cook for a minute. Deglaze the pan away from the flame with the sherry wine and cook the alcohol off (10 seconds). Add the cream sauce and bring just to simmer. Divide evenly into an ovenproof baking dish, or four welsh rarebits. Top with both cheeses and bread crumbs (I like to toss the panko in a couple tablespoons of melted butter to help brown). Place in a 475°F oven for 3–5 minutes or until cheese melts and crumbs are golden. At the restaurant we serve this with a side of English peas sautéed and tossed with scallion and bacon lardons. Enjoy!

Courtesy of Chef Brent Pilrain of Patriots Tavern (p. 169)

Balsamico Pizza

Chef's note: *I saw a chef of mine years ago make an appetizer that inspired this pizza. He brought in fresh figs one afternoon and split a crisscross on the top about an inch down, stuffed them with a very nice gorgonzola bleu cheese, and then wrapped each stuffed fig with prosciutto. We then baked them in a wood-fired oven, plated them on field greens, and drizzled aged balsamic vinegar on them. Fantastico! Here is where I took it to pizza (and I would guess I'm not the first).*

Serves 4

- 1 cup all-purpose flour
- 12 ounces fresh pizza dough (if using frozen dough balls, thaw and let proof until a slight rise occurs)
- 4 tablespoons extra-virgin olive oil
- 2 cups pizza cheese (most 4 blends will work—mozz, provolone, asiago, pecorino, etc.)
- 6–8 dried or candied packaged figs (sliced, stems removed)
- 4 ounces gorgonzola dolce (this bleu is imported from Italy, it's young, soft, and creamy)
- 8 slices prosciutto di parma (very thinly sliced)
- 1½ cups mesclun greens (spring mix or any baby field greens)
- 4 tablespoons aged balsamic vinegar (5 years or better; I like Saporoso)
- 2 tablespoons Calabrian fig molasses (may omit if too hard to find)

Dust bench or table with flour and also coat dough ball liberally. Flatten dough down by hand, working evenly around with palms of your hand and fingertips (warming the dough to body temperature helps spin a better dough). Begin

stretching gently in a circular motion until dough reaches approximate dimension of 14 inches. Drizzle half the olive oil on dough and then evenly cover with pizza cheese. Now add figs and gorgonzola by spreading around in "dollops." Pizza is ready for oven. Remove pizza from table with a pizza paddle dusted lightly with flour, and place preferably in a wood-fired oven heated to 550°F directly on the brick (also you could heat a pizza stone to 500°F; this may add a few minutes' cooking time). Turned every 30 seconds, the pizza should be bubbly and dark golden around edges in 2–3 minutes. Remove from oven and slice into 8 pieces. Top with folded prosciutto, pile greens in middle, and drizzle remaining oil, vinegar, and molasses over pizza. Balisimo!

Courtesy of Chef Brent Pilrain of Roma Restaurant (p. 170)